D1634182

ENGLISH CRITICISM OF THE NOVEL 1865–1900

ENGLISH CRITICISM OF THE NOVEL

1865-1900

BY

KENNETH GRAHAM

WITHDRAWN

OXFORD
AT THE CLARENDON PRESS

Oxford University Press, Ely House, London W. 1
GLASGOW NEW YORK TORONTO MELBOURNE WELLINGTON
CAPE TOWN SALISBURY IBADAN NAIROBI LUSAKA ADDIS ABABA
BOMBAY CALCUTTA MADRAS KARACHI LAHORE DACCA
KUALA LUMPUR HONG KONG TOKYO

© Oxford University Press 1965

FIRST PUBLISHED 1965
IN THE *Oxford English Monographs*
REPRINTED LITHOGRAPHICALLY IN GREAT BRITAIN
FROM CORRECTED SHEETS OF THE FIRST EDITION
BY WILLIAM CLOWES AND SONS, LIMITED
LONDON AND BECCLES
1966, 1967

CONTENTS

PREFACE

IN this book I have tried to illuminate an area of literary criticism which has remained largely unknown, despite the essential part it must play in any complete picture of Victorian aesthetics, or, in fact, of the Victorian novel itself. I have concentrated on the general movements of opinion, arranged according to certain broad topics, rather than give any detailed treatment of individual critics—though the reappearance of some names will, I hope, suggest lines of further enquiry. Unavoidably, some over-clarification must result from this arrangement: it should be borne in mind throughout that each of the themes separately discussed exists only within a complex system of interdependence and contradiction that can never be reproduced.

There are two other arbitrary decisions which should be explained. Henry James has been relegated to the background of this study, not out of iconoclasm, but because his criticism has been very adequately documented already. Some fresh light may be thrown on his ideas if they are seen as developments of certain contemporary strains; but above all, the criticism of these contemporaries should for once be seen in its own right, as expressing Victorian ideas about Victorian fiction and not as mere *ur*-Jamesian fumblings or non-Jamesian irrelevancies. Secondly, to take 1865 and 1900 as my boundaries is obviously artificial to some extent, and does not imply that there was any neat cohesiveness to those thirty-five years. In a general way, however, the period does have a recognizable and important character of its own, beginning as it does with the last years of mid-Victorianism, when Dickens was still alive and George Eliot dominated the scene, and going on to cover the two decades of violent literary controversy and experiment in which the Victorian age ended.

Richard Stang's *The Theory of the Novel in England, 1850–1870* appeared in 1959 when my own work was already in progress, and a few instances of overlapping have occurred; but none of these is very material, and I hope the effect will be that of following on, in a useful and slightly different way, where Professor Stang's survey left off.

Most of my material has been drawn from the pages of Victorian periodicals, which were the pulpits and platforms of their disputatious era. Contemporary letters, diaries, and memoirs do cast light on questions of literary reputations and public taste, but as regards theoretical questions they are nugatory in comparison. Most criticism published as volumes appeared first as articles, and has been referred to in that form in almost all cases, the date of this first appearance often being of some importance. Wherever known, authors of anonymous articles have been named without comment, on the authority (unless otherwise stated) of later well-known republication, or of entries in the unpublished *Wellesley Index to Victorian Periodicals*. I am extremely grateful to Professor W. E. Houghton, General Editor of the *Index*, for his kindness in this matter, and look forward like all those interested in Victorian studies to the completion of the mammoth and invaluable project to which he has devoted himself. Reviews in the *Spectator* during the years 1874–7 and 1880–1900 have been identified from editorial files by kind permission of the present Editor.

My thanks are due to the Carnegie Trust for the Universities of Scotland and the trustees of the Charles and Julia Henry Fund, whose respective awards made my researches possible; and to Mr. J. B. Bamborough, for his help and encouragement at various stages of this work.

1

THE STATUS OF FICTION

BY the mid point of the Victorian age, the art form that had produced *Emma*, *Bleak House*, and *Wuthering Heights* had still not established its full claim to legitimacy in the eyes of critics and readers. All the journals of the time questioned the phenomenon of its popularity, and recognized the immense predominance of novels as one of the controversial features of an epoch of science and social observation. 'They are the manna of the latter half of the nineteenth century', *Temple Bar* cried in 1874, with a note of panic.[1] And whether they regretted or approved, the critics found themselves discussing the credentials of fiction with a greater urgency than ever. They did so in three main ways: its moral function in society; its claims to intellectual and imaginative profundity; and the aesthetic principles of its form.

I. THE INSTRUCTOR

The puritan anxieties of mid-Victorianism were still rampant in the sixties, and until about 1880 the influence of fiction on morals and behaviour remained a genuinely burning question in certain quarters. For the *Dublin University Magazine* in 1867, for example, the influence was so real that immorality in a novel had to be seen as 'one of the greatest evils which the intellectual history of a nation can record'[2]; and the Wesleyan *London Quarterly Review* in 1866 had an almost apocalyptic vision of the whole of society crumbling under the baleful influence of

[1] 'The Novels of Miss Broughton', xli (1874), 198.
[2] 'Balzac—His Literary Labours', lxx (1867), 529.

sensation novels and the 'subtle poison' of Charles Reade, Wilkie Collins and Mrs. Henry Wood.[1] The method of the attacks—indicative of the elementary state of novel-theory at the time—is usually to leap from moral disapproval of one specific novel to alarming conclusions about the corruptive nature of the whole genre, including the almost mandatory reference to fiction's fatal effects on 'the moral fibre'. Wilkie Collins himself, smarting from being so often pilloried, gives an amusing picture of these suspicions:

If the dull people of our district were told to-morrow that my wife, daughters, and nieces had all eloped in different directions, leaving just one point of the compass open as a runaway outlet for me and the cook, I feel firmly persuaded that not one of them would be inclined to discredit the report. 'This is what comes of novel-reading!' they would say—and would return, with renewed zest, to their Voyages and Travels, their accouchements in real life, their canting 'national morality', and their blustering 'purity of hearths and homes'.[2]

Of course, many other critics applying the test of moral utility to novels are more optimistic. Some take a patriotic pride in the nation's fiction: '. . . in this branch [our country] especially excels—that from her have sprung high-minded and impartial authors of fiction, the brilliancy of whose writing is no less conspicuous than the purity of their moral teaching—that by this instrumentality education has been advanced, social abuse rectified, and virtue generally encouraged'.[3] And even the Congregationalist *British Quarterly Review* (an interesting magazine of mingled enlightenment and drab pietism) allows that such moral idealism as George MacDonald's gives fiction 'its noble place in the priesthood of letters'.[4]

In 1870, in the midst of the debate, *Tinsley's Magazine* takes a momentary stand against the tendency of its utilitarian age to look for more than amusement in fiction. But the weakness of its

[1] 'Recent Novels: their Moral and Religious Teaching', xxvii (1866), 100–24.

[2] *My Miscellanies*, 1863, i, 77.

[3] 'The Art of Novel Writing', *Gentleman's Mag.* ix, n.s. (1872), 384–93.

[4] lv (1872), 265–6.

position is revealed when it goes on unabashed to give details of how novel-reading broadens the experience, 'keeps awake a good ideal of life', 'awakens a little heroism', teaches girls 'unselfishness, and kindliness, and courtesy', and provides an education in the world for young curates.[1] And in the following year the same magazine nervously disparages even Sir Walter Scott for failing to develop fully the moral usefulness that has made fiction respectable since his time. His novels amuse, but 'they lack an object worthy of such genius and power . . . we are tempted to ask, Was there no great living truth to defend?'[2]

In the long run, the novel's status as an independent form suffered as much from these moral-utilitarian friends as from its evangelical enemies. Certainly, such naïve justifications of the art as Anthony Trollope's were hardly emancipating. He is always willing to concede that novel-reading can be an opiate and time-waster, and is obsessed with its potential dangers for women and the young, who take fiction as their vade-mecum to life. Within these limits, however, Trollope is loud in his vindication—and it is significant how even in the late seventies and after, the novel apparently needed such a moral champion. Poetry remains in his eyes the crown of the arts, but he perpetually urges a truer appreciation of the high calling of the novelist, based on the fact that his *teaching* is of the same nature as the poet's, and is directed to the same ends of honour, love, worship and humanity.[3]

One approach favoured by both sides in the debate is to judge fiction by its peculiar effect on the imagination and sensibilities of readers. In 1866 the *Saturday Review*, for example, sees this indirect influence as the novel's greatest practical merit, in view of the close link between man's 'dramatic imagination' and his whole moral nature—remarking that one alleged cause of the

[1] 'The Uses of Fiction', vi (1870), 180–5.

[2] 'The Scott Centenary', ix (1871–2), 85–86.

[3] e.g. 'On English Prose Fiction as a Rational Amusement' (1870), *Four Lectures*, ed. M. L. Parrish, 1938, pp. 94–124; 'Novel-Reading', *Nineteenth Century*, v (1879), 24–43; and *An Autobiography*, 1883, ii, 25–37 (Chapter 12). See below, p. 72.

Indian Mutiny was the lack of such imagination in the British.[1] This oblique kind of utility clearly offers a novelist—or a theorist—rather more scope than Trollope's. And it was the one celebratedly used by George Eliot to justify the importance of her profession:

> The greatest benefit we owe to the artist, whether painter, poet, or novelist, is the extension of our sympathies. . . . When Scott takes us into Luckie Mucklebackit's cottage . . . more is done towards linking the higher classes with the lower, towards obliterating the vulgarity of exclusiveness, than by hundreds of sermons and philosophical dissertations. Art is the nearest thing to life; it is a mode of amplifying experience and extending our contact with our fellow-men beyond the bounds of our personal lot.[2]

But more important than the difference from Trollope is the fact that she, too, takes her 'office of teacher or influencer of the public mind' as the key to the immense responsibility and 'sacredness of the writer's art',[3] and is unsparing in her censure of those who would betray that art's new-found seriousness.

The novel's innate appeal to the imagination can, on the other hand, arouse distrust and condemnation. Ruskin, for example, is one who always seems to have a latent fear that its effects are unavoidably enervating—and this despite his own liking for such writers as Balzac and George Sand, and despite his early defence of Bulwer and his beloved Scott from their puritan detractors.[4] In 1865 he expresses the belief that the occasional usefulness of novels as 'treatises on moral anatomy' is outweighed by the dangers: '. . . with respect to that sore temptation of novel reading, it is not the badness of a novel that we should dread, but its over-wrought interest . . . the best romance becomes dangerous if, by its excitement, it renders the ordinary

[1] 'The Uses of Fiction', xxii (1866), 323–4.

[2] 'The Natural History of German Life', *Westminster Rev.* x, n.s. (1856), 54. For more on this moral-imaginative effect, see below, pp. 79–81.

[3] 'Leaves from a Note-Book', *Essays*, ed. C. L. Lewes, 1884, p. 358; and 'Silly Novels by Lady Novelists', *Westminster Rev.* x, n.s. (1856), 460.

[4] 'Essay on Literature—1836', *Works*, Library Edn., 1903–12, i, 357–75; and *passim*.

course of life uninteresting, and increases the morbid thirst for useless acquaintance with scenes in which we shall never be called upon to act.'[1]

Discussions of the novel's moral usefulness decline noticeably after 1880. Many critics, no doubt, would still subscribe fundamentally to Trollope's or George Eliot's position, but the need to be so defensive is no longer felt. Articles with a moralistic bent still abound, but are much less concerned with the basic justification of novel-writing or novel-reading as one of the activities of mankind. When a novel is attacked for not observing the moral code, the critic now takes it for granted that it could be written *better*, instead of deducing that the whole genre is inferior. In addition, the growing respectability of fiction is confirmed in the eighties and nineties by the novelist's new position in society, the minutiae of his life and opinions being reported in every gossip-column and in such new periodicals as *The Bookman* and *Literature*, and his vocation thoroughly professionalized by the activities of dedicated organizers like Walter Besant.[2]

However, it would be misleading to suggest that the novel had won complete moral respect by 1880, as the older attitude continues to crop up in various articles, mainly as a minor element in them. For example, even Besant's *The Art of Fiction* (1884), which is largely an attempt to boost the novel's status on the grounds of its formal laws and technical demands, makes much of its qualifications as a universal teacher of 'life and manners, of philosophy and art; even of science and religion',

[1] *Sesame and Lilies*, 1865, p. 163. This pronouncement is a perfect expression of the old Benthamite and religious attitudes: for example, it echoes exactly an attack by the *Christian Observer* for 1815 quoted in R. D. Altick, *The English Common Reader*, Chicago, 1957, pp. 110–11.

[2] Besant's *The Pen and the Book* (1899) gives a valuable account of the rise to social acceptance and commercial security of 'the Literary Life', and of the commendable motives which inspired him to play such a notable part: 'I have endeavoured to make my readers understand that this kind of work should be regarded as a career worthy of the highest honour and respect: that it should be taken in hand most seriously and earnestly, and with due regard to the responsibilities of the work.' (p. vii.)

its preaching of a high morality, and its enlivening of the sense of sympathy.[1] And Mrs. Craik in 1882, and Henry Norman in 1883, still describe the importance and responsibility of the novelist in terms of his capacity to corrupt the nation's youth and lead our daughters down the primrose path of 'forbidden topics': the future of the art is one of guidance, instruction, and the saving of souls.[2] Outright denunciation of the whole form is much less common: one example from *Blackwood's* as late as 1898 is enough to record an outdated, though perennial, cast of mind. The writer, after finding some merit in contemporary fiction, suspects dolefully that all novel-reading is in the end 'enervating and debilitating rather than bracing and tonic; that instead of building up character upon the solid foundation of principle, it runs it up on the rickety foundation of emotion; and that, far from fortifying the reader for the trials and vicissitudes of life, it saps such resolution and firmness as he may already possess'.[3]

Apart from such exceptions, however, this part of the battle was really over. By 1880 'Henry Holbeach' (W. B. Rands) could express his amazement at the novel's rapid rise to respectability over the previous twenty years and, with some confidence, describe its remaining moral detractors as a small and unimportant band of 'the Evangelical'.[4] The debate on the novel's status continued—but the issue had changed.

II. THE ENTERTAINER

Mid-Victorian critics of fiction anxious for their subject's prestige could hardly be expected to stress its undoubted ability to entertain. Rather, the need was to defend it from those who insisted it could do little more. During the sixties and seventies,

[1] pp. 8–9. See also his 'The Value of Fiction', *Belgravia*, xvi (1872), 48–51.

[2] Mrs. Craik, *Plain Speaking*, 1882, pp. 173–7; Henry Norman, 'Theories and Practice of Modern Fiction', *Fortnightly Rev.* xxxiv, n.s. (1883), 883–6.

[3] 'Among the Young Lions', clxiii (1898), 742 (by J. H. Millar).

[4] 'The New Fiction', *Contemporary Rev.* xxxvii (1880), 247–62.

as we have seen, the higher function most commonly suggested was that of moral profit, the possible contradictions between this and entertainment being quietly glossed over. And even from such critics, there is a large measure of depreciation on intellectual grounds. For example, the youthful Edward Dowden in 1865 suggests the cultivation of sympathy as a justification for fiction, yet asserts that its first function is to relax and amuse, best achieved when the reader is resting after work and under the age of twenty-five.[1] And a more outright contempt is often expressed in such terms as *Temple Bar*'s in 1870, that 'novels, *quâ* novels, are not peculiarly an intellectual exercise, either for the reader or the writer of them',[2] and in the *Saturday*'s, three years later, that 'it is a natural impression that the habit of endless story-telling and endless story-reading is hardly likely to encourage strenuous thought . . . it is perhaps demoralizing in the sense of softening the intellectual fibre'.[3]

From the beginning, a number of critics tried to counter this prevalent attitude by a new emphasis not on the morally uplifting but on the intellectual and imaginative elements of the novel. In 1867 the *British Quarterly Review* sets its sights high, and praises fiction for its comprehensiveness that embraces the functions of epic, drama, and lyric. What can the novelist *not* achieve? the writer wonders. The highest truths—as distinct from mere moral lessons—can be arrived at through fiction, especially when in the hands of George Eliot, whose high seriousness is compared to Goethe's.[4] And two years later the *Leader*, less optimistic, regrets that the low standards of contemporary fiction should conceal the fact that 'the novel proper deserves to be regarded with as much reverence as any choice work of art, making demands upon the head which the highest works in other departments—the historical, the critical, the biographical—would dismally fail to supply'.[5]

[1] 'Fiction and its Uses', *Fraser's Mag.* lxxii (1865), 746–51.
[2] 'Our Novels. The Simple School', xxix (1870), 488–503.
[3] 'Mr. Trollope on Novels', xxxvi (1873), 656–7.
[4] 'George Eliot', xlv (1867), 141–3.
[5] iii (1869), 252.

After this early skirmishing, the major campaign in favour of the novel's intellectual eminence came with all the suddenness of a revolution—one of the major revolutions of Victorian criticism. George Meredith was a name particularly associated with it, and two articles on his work, in 1879, pointed the way. In one, the *Saturday* welcomes *The Egoist* on the very grounds of its difficulty, since this toughness disturbs the customary idea, created by the mass of soporific fiction, that novel-reading is an unintellectual purging of the passions, usually in a context of 'armchairs, pipes, and slippers'.[1] And in the *British Quarterly Review* appears an almost Shelleyan manifesto of the potentialities of fiction, inspired by Meredith's own high achievements in it. The novel, according to this writer, has supplanted poetry and the drama as 'the interpreter of thought and feeling and passion, the teacher of the lessons of life, the mirror of humanity', and gives us not just a picture of outward manners, but of the very springs of action and philosophy. Without needing to preach, the novel can attain to the highest attributes of poetry:

> It may be true to its object of giving us the external aspects of human life, of setting forth those moral and social phenomena we have spoken of; may delight us with characters so painted that fiction becomes reality; and may yet attune our minds to the music of the spheres. . . . Writing as one who aims always at discerning and being true to the deeper, underlying truth of things, [the novelist] will show you the meaning of those phenomena; he will reflect not only the thought of the age, but will prepare our minds for the thought of the future.[2]

From this time on, 'seriousness' and 'thought' become the key-words in the aims of a whole new generation of novelists and critics—the heirs, it is often said, to a movement that George Eliot had begun. Men like Meredith, Hardy, Moore, and Gissing become the centres of various storms, both through their own statements on the high art of fiction and the critical

[1] xlviii (1879), 607–8.

[2] 'The Novels of George Meredith', lxix (1879), 411–13 (by Arabella Shore).

cults that grew—and clashed—around them. The concept of the novel as mere entertainment has to be combated once again; and the idea of moral utility, far from being offered as an acceptable makeweight to entertainment, is now seen as a facet of prudery, and hence itself a major obstacle to the novel's development. Mrs. Grundy, together with the slippered reader in search of amusement, have found their most eloquent enemies. 'Brainstuff', 'philosophy', and 'the Idea' are what the novel should embody, in Meredith's eyes, rather than inculcate bourgeois morality on the one hand or kill time on the other.[1] And Moore, the great flayer of his contemporaries, explains angrily: 'My concern is not with those who look upon literature as another form of bicycling.'[2] 'Artistic Conscience' is another of the rallying-cries. In 1884 Gissing, for example, impressed like the others by the self-respect and seriousness of the French and Russian novelists, attacks the stranglehold of popular demand and the Circulating Library: 'English novels are miserable stuff for a very miserable reason, simply because English novelists fear to do their best lest they should damage their popularity, and consequently their income. . . . Let novelists be true to their artistic conscience, and the public taste will come round.'[3] For the first time in its history, the novel had become conceived of as a refuge for the intelligentsia and an organ of advanced thinking.

The idea was furthered not simply by the writers whom we would most esteem today, but by all those minor figures who caused the sudden proliferation after 1880 of the so-called 'novel of ideas': names like J. H. Shorthouse, Mrs. Humphry Ward, Mark Rutherford, Olive Schreiner, Grant Allen, Sarah Grand, Edna Lyall—even Marie Corelli and Hall Caine. No matter how inferior the performance, the intellectual ambitions behind such works as Shorthouse's *John Inglesant* (1881) and

[1] See below, p. 74.

[2] 'A Tragic Novel', *Cosmopolis*, vii (1897), 58. See also 'Since the Elizabethans', ibid. iv (1896), 42–58.

[3] 'The New Censorship of Literature', letter to the *Pall Mall Gazette*, xl (15 December 1884), 2.

Mrs. Ward's *Robert Elsmere* (1888) gave the novel the status of a widely-heard participator in most of the great religious, social, philosophic, and scientific controversies of the day—and the two in question brought Mr. Gladstone himself into the ranks of novel-critics, as champion of the one, and severe opponent of the other.[1] The effect was evident through the whole field of fiction and fiction-reviewing. Even Julia Wedgwood (one of the *Contemporary*'s least prophetic reviewers) was able by 1886 to grasp the revolution that was taking place around her: 'Perhaps the most marked characteristic of the fiction of our day, as compared with the fiction of our fathers, is its ambitious character. To them it was the diversion of an idle hour, the repository of their lighter fancies; to us it is the vehicle of almost all thought for which a large audience is desired.'[2]

The idea of the novel as pure entertainment died hard, nevertheless. In fact, about this time there is a mild reaction against the new seriousness of 'light literature', and some protesters turn in relief to the fare offered by the new school of romance. Mrs. Oliphant in 1884 questions Besant's recent 'elevated ideas concerning fiction as an art', and sees it, rather, as 'one of the alleviations of life', which she herself indulges in mostly when in bed with a cold[3]; and Edmund Gosse in 1892, while appreciative of the pleasure novels afford, implies that it is usually in a man's weaker moments, when the mind is fatigued.[4] The view is often found in the writings of the many Gentlemen-Scholars who graced the end of the century, perhaps most notoriously in Andrew Lang, whose lifelong attitude of 'More claymores, less psychology' typified the undercurrent of disparagement (often unconscious) which never quite disappeared.[5]

History was clearly against the Andrew Langs. H. G. Wells,

[1] For a general account of the impact made by these books on society, see Amy Cruse, *After the Victorians*, 1938, pp. 27–36.

[2] xlix (1886), 593.

[3] 'Three Young Novelists', '*Blackwood's Edinburgh Mag*. cxxxvi (1884), 296–7.

[4] 'The Tyranny of the Novel', *National Rev*. xix (1892), 166–8.

[5] On Lang, see Malcolm Elwin, *Old Gods Falling*, 1939, pp. 190–1.

speaking in 1911, looked back on the turn of the century as having witnessed the downfall of 'the Weary Giant theory of the novel'—that fiction should provide escape and 'cooling refreshment' for the tired professional man.[1] Certainly, the novel's intellectual prestige had been transformed within a few decades, and it is this remarkable change which deserves to be emphasized. But in Wells's day, and even in our own, the apotheosis was far from complete. In 1958 Margaret Kennedy could still refer to novelists, in the title of her book, as Outlaws on Parnassus—and if they *are* still in exile, in the eyes of a few, it is through the same old prejudice against the motley of the public entertainer.

III. THE ART-FORM

More strictly aesthetic matters were also important in determining the status of fiction: for example, the attitude of critics to the general nature of its form; the recognition of its independence as a genre, with its own laws and theory; and the need for it to maintain certain standards of workmanship.

As for the first of these, the idea is sometimes expressed, especially in the earlier years, that no matter how the formal elements of the novel are to be defined, they will always be in some degree un-aesthetic by their very nature. For example, George Barnett Smith in 1874 bestows high praise on Fielding, but adds: 'The novel will never be able to assume a position of equal importance with the drama, because of its comparative defectiveness of construction',[2] apparently believing, like many of his contemporaries, that the novel's looseness of structure could be judged against the requirements of an entirely different art, and not according to its own ends. Others, however, like the author of 'Novels and Novelists' in the *Saturday Review* for 1872, accepts the flexibility of the novel as a

[1] 'The Contemporary Novel', in *An Englishman Looks at the World*, 1914, pp. 148–9.

[2] 'Our First Great Novelist', *Macmillan's Mag.* xxx (1874), 1.

valid aesthetic merit: 'Of all forms of literary art, the novel is the one which lends itself with the greatest facility to the expression of every possible variety of emotion'—though the temptations and dangers of this laxity are admitted.[1]

By the eighties there is much less questioning of fiction's eligibility to be an art on formal grounds. Vernon Lee's objections of this kind are unusual, and are largely contradicted by her own fruitful enquiries elsewhere into the structure of the novel.[2] On at least two occasions, however, she claims that it is only a half-art, compared with painting or music, since it lacks the means to convert its subject-matter of human, moral concerns into those particular sense-impressions which constitute 'the beautiful'. Its attractions are mainly non-aesthetic: the logical appeal of argument, the gaining of a knowledge of life, emotional excitement, and the satisfaction that comes from complex patterns of words. Only the latter, of course, might be called form in the novel, and Vernon Lee claims that it can get by without such a quality, appealing to its readers usually in their more practical moments and capacities.[3]

Most critics had no such doubts, and were in various ways preparing the ground for a fuller acceptance of the novel as an independent and internally regulated art-form. Definition was an obvious need, but there are few if any attempts to go beyond the traditional concept of a 'prose epic' based on truth to nature, regular development of plot, and 'something of the dramatic element' added.[4] There is a fairly common inability to distinguish between fiction and history, or biography—a familiar difficulty in early novel-theory—especially where a historical or a foreign novel is concerned. Informativeness of any kind is enough to ensure many pseudo-novels serious critical attention, especially when the facts are about Life in Our Colonies, and the approach often obscures proper consideration of more worth-

[1] xxxiii (1872), 722–3. [2] See below, pp. 135–9.

[3] 'The Aesthetics of the Novel', *Literature*, v (1899), 98–100. See also her 'A Dialogue on Novels', *Contemporary Rev.* xlviii (1885), 384–8.

[4] e.g. 'On the History of the Novel in England', *Argosy*, xiv (1872), 273.

while writers. For example, one of the most recurrent themes of articles on Turgenev is seen in R. F. Littledale's words on *Virgin Soil*: '. . . it has an interest and value beyond that of narrative and style . . . namely, that it is an account . . . of the political condition of Russia'[1]; and Kipling, similarly, is often valued mainly as a recorder of facts about Anglo-Indian society.[2]

At times, however, some reviewers are alert to the confusion. The *Contemporary*, for example, denies the name of 'novel' to Henry Kingsley's *Mademoiselle Mathilde* in 1868 because of its excessive closeness to historical events: 'Give us history, or biography, or fiction, but do not attempt to unite the charm of fact with the charm of illusion.'[3] And again, in 1869 T. A. Trollope's *Leonora Casaloni* is criticized for following the 'founded-on-fact' fallacy: biography and fiction are based on two entirely different kinds of knowledge, the writer argues, and to become the latter, fact must be passed through the solvent of the imagination.[4] One successful fusion, according to the *Westminster* in 1887, is F. Marion Crawford's *Saracinesca*. The picture of Rome's nobility in this book is praised for its own interest: 'But the real interest of a novel can never lie in the information which it incidentally affords on any extrinsic topic. A novel is not an explanatory diagram nor a chart; but, like a picture, it is a work of art, and it must be judged successful or the reverse in proportion to its power of depicting character and presenting truly and forcibly the play of human passions.'[5]

Much more evident is the growing demand for a formal exposition of the theory of novel-writing, and for its stricter observance by critics and by authors. Although there were many like the *British Quarterly* reviewer who in 1867 believed that the essence (and value) of the novel lay in its very indefinability and lack of any possible theory (anyone can write a thing

[1] *Academy*, xiv (1878), 263.

[2] e.g. 'The Works of Mr. Rudyard Kipling', *Edinburgh Rev*. clxxxvii (1898), 206–7.

[3] ix (1868), 633–4.

[4] *Contemporary Rev*. xi (1869), 466–7.

[5] cxxviii (1887), 517.

called a novel: a novelist is really just a *man*),[1] there was also, from the very first years, a strong body of opinion on the other side. G. H. Lewes, in the *Fortnightly*, argues that the novel deserves the most rigorous standards of criticism, and would benefit from their application.[2] 'H. Lawrenny' (Edith Simcox), in the *Academy* for 1871, regrets the lack of principles in the appreciation of fiction, and wishes that Lessing were alive 'to expound the laws of romance' in such a way that the artistic profligacy of so talented a writer as Meredith might be prevented.[3] And even Trollope, whose mechanical methods and references to the novelist as a cobbler aroused such criticism when his autobiography was published in 1883, was in his way a lifelong upholder of craftsmanship, the need for training and industry, and the desirability of following 'rules for the writing of novels'.[4]

The wish for the novel to be more strict with itself, and to achieve its potentially high place in the arts, results in the endless attacks on the carelessness and mass-production of contemporary novels which is so remarkable a feature of the period's criticism. The *Westminster* in 1867 ends such a lament: 'These remarks show how high a form of art we consider the novel to be. . . . The average novel is simply an abortion'[5]; and in 1872 it holds up the painstaking methods of Hawthorne as an example of care: 'Few writers understand that a novel is as much a work of art as a poem.'[6] But there always remains a very British prejudice against prescription and exact codification, which results in some awkward contradictions with the desire for good workmanship. Examples of this confusion are provided by writers in the *Saturday Review*. In 1868 the competent mediocrity of Mrs. Craik's *Mildred* is regretted: 'We cannot help wondering more and more deeply, as we read more and more novels, why

[1] xliv (1867), 142.

[2] 'Criticism in Relation to Novels', iii (1865–6), 352–61.

[3] ii (1871), 552–4.

[4] e.g. *An Autobiography*, ii, 45–62 (Chapter 12); and *Letters*, ed. B. A. Booth, London, 1951, p. 57.

[5] xxxii, n.s. (1867), 593.

[6] xlii, n.s. (1872), 544.

the writers should so systematically abstain, as their books amply prove them to have done, from the study of anything like a complete theory of fiction.'[1] And in 1874 fiction is unfavourably compared with painting for its lack of official standards: 'Now what is clearly required, so as to give the novelist the same advantages as the artist, is an Institute of Novel-Writing. There, under the guidance of professors, students would learn, not certainly to write an original work—for originality cannot be taught—but to make a composition which should not be in glaring violation of all principles of good taste.'[2] Yet in 1870 the same periodical reviews Lady Fullerton's *Mrs. Gerald's Niece* in this way:

That there should be any fixed principles for novel-writing is a long-exploded error. The literature which describes the life and manners of men must be as various as men's lives are, and all that the critic can fairly require in products of this libertine and freakish art is that they should represent faithfully some fact of human character, or at least reflect fairly some temper of the period. So fiction may range from the *Golden Legend* to *Guy Livingstone*, from *Candide* to *Mrs. Gerald's Niece*.[3]

The same contradictory tendency can be seen in the writings of George Saintsbury. Though his attitude to the novel is often one of well-bred academic condescension, he is a perpetual champion of the diligence required by the art, and the necessity for standards to be upheld. In 1874 he reviews G. Cameron's *Charlie Lufton*: 'Mr. Cameron has yet to learn (for the matter of that so have thousands of other people) that novel writing, so far from being appropriate to a *coup d'essai*, is about the hardest of all tasks which an author can set himself'[4]; and in his years with the *Academy* he continually attacks wilfulness and lack of conscientiousness in authors. Yet in 1887 Saintsbury indulges in one of his insular sneers at the excess of theorizing in America, preferring the natural 'literary breeding' of Englishmen[5]; and

[1] xxvi (1868), 303–4.
[2] xxxvii (1874), 415–16.
[3] xxix (1870), 388–90.
[4] *Academy*, vi (1874), 479.
[5] 'The Present State of the Novel. I', *Fortnightly Rev.* xlii, n.s. (1887), 412.

five years later he expresses annoyance at modern young writers' devotion to such 'secondary and subsidiary matters' as style and formal construction. Unlike poetry, he believes, form is not part of the novel's essence, and while it is a pity that a novel should not be written carefully according to principles of construction, the fault is not a fatal one, as many of the greatest novels have shown.[1]

By the eighties, however, a far more consistent advocacy of technical care and proficiency arose, revolving, most notably, around the names of Moore, Stevenson, Gissing—and, of course, Henry James. On the model of Flaubert, each was a self-conscious martyr to technique. Moore's endless rewriting in a quest for verbal perfection became legendary; and Gissing, who compares the freedom of Dickens and Scott with the exacting standards of his own day—'our grave Art of Fiction, a bitter task-mistress'[2]—gives ample testimony throughout his letters and diary of his own devotion to the new goddess. 'Wrote from 3 to 9 but with no results: it must all be cancelled. . . . My patience is inexhaustible', he notes in 1888. And again: 'The first volume I am re-writing for at least the fifth time, and, for a wonder, I feel tolerably satisfied.'[3]

The famous agonies of Stevenson emphasize even more clearly how, for these writers, the novel had become an art in which excellence was to be pursued with religious fanaticism. The old utilitarian justification is never completely out of Stevenson's Calvinist mind[4]; but it is much more by an insistence on form that he vindicates his high conception of his art, recommending as the ideal towards which the novitiate must strive, 'those more exquisite refinements of proficiency and

[1] 'The Present State of the English Novel, 1892', *Miscellaneous Essays*, 1892, pp. 412–18. His scepticism as to the value of technique in fiction is given its fullest expression in 'Technique', *Dial*, New York, lxxx (1926), 273–8.

[2] *Charles Dickens*, 1898, pp. 48–49.

[3] *Letters of George Gissing to Members of his Family*, ed. A. and E. Gissing, 1927, p. 206.

[4] See 'The Morality of the Profession of Letters', *Fortnightly Rev.* xxix, n.s. (1881), 513–20.

finish . . . for which, day after day, he recasts and revises and rejects'.[1] The rule he lays down in 1883 for the writer, as for 'the student of any art', might be taken as the quintessence of formalist devotion, and as representing one particular peak in the history of the status of fiction:

An art is the very gist of life; it grows with you; you will never weary of an art at which you fervently and superstitiously labour . . . forget the world in a technical trifle.

. . . In your own art, bow your head over technique. Think of technique when you rise and when you go to bed. Forget purposes in the meanwhile; get to love technical processes; to glory in technical successes; get to see the world entirely through technical spectacles, to see it entirely in terms of what you can do. Then when you have anything to say, the language will be apt and copious.[2]

From the eighties onwards, a new enthusiasm and confidence are expressed stridently by critics and reviewers. The greater expertise of the French is constantly being held up as a reproach to the native product, which reveals only too clearly its lack of theoretical principles and canons of criticism, as well as the need for the novelist to be trained in his art like a painter or a sculptor.[3] Walter Besant's 1884 lecture, *The Art of Fiction*, indignantly attacks the society that still regards the novel with 'affectionate contempt' and stresses that it is the complete equal of the other arts, regulated like them by laws as exact and as teachable as those of harmony. And the hostile reactions which this idea drew only helped to stimulate the debate.[4] By 1890 detailed discussion and controversy over aims, methods, and principles had become such a feature of the literary scene that J. A. Noble in the *Spectator* commends 'a writer like Mr.

[1] 'Letter to a Young Gentleman Who Proposes to Embrace the Career of Art' (1888), in *Across the Plains*, 1892, pp. 272–88.

[2] *Letters*, ed. S. Colvin, 1911, ii, 125.

[3] e.g. Henry Holbeach (i.e. W. B. Rands), 'The New Fiction', *Contemporary Rev.* xxxvii (1880), 247; and Henry Norman, 'Theories and Practice of Modern Fiction', *Fortnightly Rev.* xxxiv, n.s. (1883), 870–5.

[4] See R. H. Hutton's hostility in the *Spectator*, 'Mr. Besant on the Art of Fiction', lvii (1884), 674–5; and James Purves's scorn for 'Mr. Besant's recipe' in 'Mr. Thomas Hardy's Rustics', *Time*, i, n.s. (1885), 715–16.

James Payn, who has never given a lecture or written a magazine article on the subject of his art'[1]; and J. M. Barrie indulges in the humorous little fantasy of 'Brought Back from Elysium', in which the shades of Scott, Fielding, Smollett, Dickens, and Thackeray, after being harangued by a modern Realist, a Romancist, an 'Elsmerian', and a Stylist, representatives of current cliques, take their leave with a dignified exhortation to think and write less about styles and theories and concentrate on the business in hand.[2]

Nevertheless, the critics and theorizers were undeterred, and their various battles raged on. That they found the novel worth fighting over was the important thing, as Henry James pointed out in 1884, in the eloquent vindication he offered for their efforts:

> . . . within a year or two . . . the era of discussion would appear to have been to a certain extent opened. Art lives upon discussion, upon experiment, upon curiosity, upon variety of attempt, upon the exchange of views and the comparison of standpoints. . . . The successful application of any art is a delightful spectacle, but the theory, too, is interesting; and though there is a great deal of the latter without the former, I suspect there has never been a genuine success that has not had a latent core of conviction.[3]

This 'core of conviction'—the established status of the novel—is a product of all the detailed disputes over realism, morality, and technique to which we must now turn.

[1] lxiv (1890), 919–20. Payn was not entirely inarticulate: see below, pp. 77–8, 126.

[2] *Contemporary Rev.* lvii (1890), 846–54.

[3] 'The Art of Fiction', *Longman's Mag.* iv (1884), 502–3.

2

THE QUESTION OF REALISM

THANKS to Plato, mimesis stands like a dragon at the gate in any discussion of aesthetics—and particularly so as regards the novel, the most apparently mimetic of the arts. Those who presided over its birth in the eighteenth century made authenticity their central creed, while some theorists of the twentieth century have so concentrated on its use of convention, symbol, and myth that the idea of simple correspondence with the 'real' world has been lost. Somewhere between the two come the Victorians, agitated, questioning, uncomfortably transitional as always. They were devotees of the daguerreotype, and flocked to see Frith's *Derby Day* in the Royal Academy.[1] But it is quite wrong to suggest (as is done so often) that their theory of fiction was quite dominated by this kind of realism. The belief that the novel is a 'slice of life'—or at least that it reflects objectively and in a factual way the more ordinary aspects of human experience—is certainly important in the thinking of the age. But we shall have to give attention to various important concepts that go against this tendency: the pleasure that is provided only by an artificial selection out of life's material, for example; the allowance for subjectivity in the act of writing; the belief that art penetrates to a new, transcendental order of reality; or the acceptance of pattern and convention as a technical necessity. These ideas are in constant dialectic with the principle of realism. And when the last two decades of the century see the rise of a new school of realism and a rival school of romance, dialectic turns to warfare.

[1] For a general account of realism in Victorian taste, see J. H. Buckley, *The Victorian Temper*, London, 1952, pp. 133-8.

I. A MIRROR OF LIFE

The attitude favouring realism takes many forms, naïve or less naïve, but rarely produces a comprehensive theory. It is a general emphasis, a way of thinking, that influences the whole climate of critical opinion; and in George Eliot and Trollope it finds perhaps its best-known representatives.

The major theme running through all George Eliot's comments on her art is the necessity to avoid exaggeration, conventionality, and all literary affectation; and by the canon of simple veracity she tries and condemns countless inferior novels in her criticism for the *Westminster* and the *Leader* in the fifties. Reviewing Ruskin's *Modern Painters* in the former, she observes: 'The truth of infinite value that he teaches is *realism*—the doctrine that all truth and beauty are to be attained by a humble and faithful study of nature, and not by substituting vague forms, bred by imagination on the mists of feeling, in place of definite, substantial reality.'[1] Her two most important essays, 'The Natural History of German Life' and 'Silly Novels by Lady Novelists', repeat her objections to the affected and the unreal[2]; and in 1859 her famous defence of realism in Chapter 17 of *Adam Bede* shows the simplicity and strength of her mimetic view: 'So I am content to tell my simple story, without trying to make things seem better than they were; dreading nothing, indeed, but falsity, which, in spite of one's best efforts, there is reason to dread. Falsehood is so easy, truth so difficult. . . . It is for this rare, precious quality of truthfulness that I delight in many Dutch paintings, which lofty-minded people despise.'[3]

Apart from the moral qualifications, on which she was highly articulate, George Eliot had little more to say on representation in the novel that is not merely eloquent repetition of this creed. No matter how unlike her own novels were to the simple mirror-image—for example in their use of convention and the devices of

[1] ix, n.s. (1856), 626.

[2] *Westminster Rev.* x, n.s. (1856), 51–79; and 442–61.

[3] Cabinet Edn., n.d., i, 267–8.

melodrama, as well as the subjectivity of much of their treatment—her actual critical opinions paid little attention to the distorting effects of the imagination or of the novel's structural demands, and in her own mind she seems to have remained as straightforward a realist as most of her ordinary readers.[1]

Trollope is the High Priest of Victorian realism, in theory as in practice. 'Realistic', 'truthful', and 'natural' are his favourite words of commendation; ordinary human nature is always held up as the lodestar of the novelist; and the ancient charge that all fictions are lies is to be answered simply by the writer's ability to be factually correct.[2] Hence, he frequently defends the lack of heroics in his own novels by reference to everyday experience: 'Oh, thou, my reader, whose sympathies are in truth the great and only aim of my work, when you have called the dearest of your friends round you to your hospitable table, how many heroes are there sitting at the board?'[3] And in welcoming Hawthorne's praise for his realism, he makes clear his essential credo: 'I have always desired to "hew out some lump of the earth", and to make men and women walk upon it just as they do walk here among us,—with not more of excellence, nor with exaggerated baseness,—so that my readers might recognise human beings like to themselves.'[4]

At times, Trollope does show some response to other modes than the realistic, admiring Hawthorne's imaginative sublimity and even accepting the existence of a sensational element in all novels.[5] And in his *Thackeray* (1879), he admits that the realistic

[1] G. H. Lewes, who was far from a straightforward realist, may have influenced her novels, but hardly her conscious theory. See A. R. Kaminsky, 'George Eliot, George Henry Lewes, and the Novel', *P.M.L.A.* lxx (1955), 997–1013; and below, p. 35 n. Richard Stang gives a fuller and somewhat different account of George Eliot in *The Theory of the Novel in England, 1850–1870*, London, 1959, pp. 160–6.

[2] *An Autobiography*, 1883, ii, 60–61 (Chapter 12); 'On English Prose Fiction as a Rational Amusement' (1870), *Four Lectures*, ed. M. L. Parrish, 1938, pp. 112–13.

[3] *The Eustace Diamonds*, The Oxford Trollope, 1950, i, 318–20 (Chapter 35).

[4] *An Autobiography*, i, 193–4 (Chapter 8).

[5] 'The Genius of Nathaniel Hawthorne', *North American Rev.* cxxix (1879), 204–7; and *Four Lectures*, pp. 123–4.

in art—'by which we mean that which shall seem to be real'—is different from the true-to-life, and lies somewhere between naturalism and complete artificiality.[1] But like George Eliot, he is not really concerned with the possibilities of the sublime in fiction, or with the nature of illusion. The earthbound is most suited to his taste, and his enthusiasm is reserved for simple recognizability of drawing—for the outward effects rather than the analysable causes of realism in the novel.

It can be assumed that this unsophisticated viewpoint was shared by many of his public. Frederick Locker-Lampson is typical of what the intelligent un-literary reader sought, and found, in a Trollope novel: 'Trollope's chief excellence is in the portrayal of character; the dialogue is what people naturally use; it is even more than that—they could not well use any other. I am fond of his heroines; they are affectionate and true; one knows pretty well what they are going to do next, one always feels safe with them.'[2] Other writers can explain their preference for realism in more grandiose terms than this. The *Zeitgeist*, for example, is a great favourite: that is, if the prevailing tendency of thought in the century is scientific and materialistic, then the realist novel must be bowed to as its most fitting expression. And by others, the growth of realism in character and incident since the eighteenth century is seen to be linked with the whole progress and evolution of civilization. But Locker-Lampson's simple point about Trollope's young ladies is much more firmly based. Truth to human nature is one of the most widespread and durable critical principles of the age. 'Not true-to-life', 'blurred', 'indistinct', and 'caricatures' are perpetually recurrent phrases of condemnation; and 'mixed' or 'well-rounded' characters become a reviewers' fetish. Dickens, his popularity by now declining, is often in the pillory. His characters are criticized as 'speaking abstractions or animated machines', compared with Jane Austen's or Mrs. Gaskell's, or with the more accurate 'photography' of Thackeray, or the 'sound, detailed, substantial

[1] pp. 184–6.
[2] *My Confidences*, 1896, p. 334.

completeness of sculpture' of Trollope.[1] And his influence is blamed for the way in which the 'Sensation School' draws 'characteristics' rather than 'character', mere puppets instead of 'living' figures like George Eliot's Tito Melema.[2] Continually through the earlier years, and sporadically in the eighties and nineties, it is hammered home that the essential power of any novelist 'is the capacity of representing human nature, of creating any figure without life, which to all who see it shall seem to have life, and life of the vivid kind'.[3] And 'life' is judged among such critics simply by how the character conforms to the normal patterns and motivations of everyday life.

From this touchstone there arises a characteristic of reviews that by its sheer persistence becomes an established law: that is, the appraisal of characters in a novel as 'our real-life acquaintances'. Some critics discussed, say, the 'living' effect of Dickens's characters, and recognized the illusion as a contrived effect, a quality of a different world from the everyday; but for many others, 'realism' of characterization resulted almost literally in an addition to the country's population. For example, the *British Quarterly Review* in 1868 praises the characters of Gogol because they become living people, not just portraits. They develop independently of their creator in such a way that we feel we know facts about their lives which Gogol has forgotten to give us.[4] Trollope is continually made into a fount of plenty in this respect, and his novels are for many critics a world of new friends in which it is just as natural to wonder whether poor Lily Dale will find her future life dull as a spinster as it was for Dickens's audience to plead for the life of Smike or

[1] 'The Domestic Novel', *Argosy*, xviii (1874), 295; 'Light Literature', *Belgravia*, xx (1873), 331; 'The Novels of Mr. Anthony Trollope', *Dublin Rev.* xix (1872), 396.

[2] 'Our Novels. The Sensational School', *Temple Bar*, xxix (1870), 419–20. There is an interesting examination of how Dickens's reputation suffered from the new taste for realism between 1848 and 1872 in G. H. Ford, *Dickens and his Readers*, Princeton, 1955, pp. 129–55.

[3] *Spectator*, xxxviii (1865), 1438–9.

[4] 'Nicholas Gógol', xlvii (1868), 332–3 (by C. E. Turner).

Little Nell. In 1890 H. Schütz Wilson devotes a very familiar type of article, 'Colonel Newcome', to the emotional re-creation and expansion of the character, punctuated by apostrophes; and it might be taken as typical of this kind of criticism at its extreme: 'How living, and how real, are all Thackeray's characters! We seem to see them, to look into their eyes, to hear their voices, and to comprehend their natures. We live with them with delight, and we part from them with sorrow.' [1]

The idea, of course, is found at its most unrestrained in the general reader of no great critical pretensions. Such a one is the publisher John Blackwood, who, after reading Book One of *Middlemarch* in manuscript, tells George Eliot of his anxiety as to how Dorothea will fare 'when she wakens to real life'; and, of Book Four, his wish that 'Mrs. Garth had given Caleb a thump on the side of the head when he proposed to take Fred Vincy as his assistant'.[2] And then there is the old lady, perhaps as typical of her fellow-readers today as she was ninety years ago, who lay awake all night after reading of Bulstrode and the death of Raffles: 'Poor dear creature, after he had done so much for the wretch, sitting up at night and attending on him! *and I don't believe it was the brandy that killed him*: and what is to become of Bulstrode now—he has nobody left but Christ.' [3]

But the effect was also an important criterion among the literati. To create permanent, living acquaintances, 'more real to us than Mr. and Mrs. Jones who live in the next square', is for William Mackay in 1870 the highest achievement of the artist[4]; and *The Times* in 1876 congratulates Trollope: 'The capacity for making your characters so life-like that your readers grow into their intimacy and are always eager to meet them again, seems to us one of the surest tests of a really gifted novelist.'[5] Walter Besant in 1884 enshrines it among his tablets

[1] *Gentleman's Mag.* cclxviii (1890), 497–509.

[2] *George Eliot Letters*, ed. G. S. Haight, New Haven, 1954–5, v, 148–9; 255.

[3] Quoted by Amy Cruse, *The Victorians and their Books*, 1935, pp. 283–4.

[4] 'The Late Charles Dickens', *New Monthly Mag.* cxlvii (1870), 87–88.

[5] 18 August 1876, p. 4.

of the law[1]; and finally, the *Spectator* takes the everyday realism of Mrs. Oliphant in 1892 as an occasion to formalize its critical practice:

Humanity has a faculty prompting it instinctively to criticise the behaviour of its neighbours, and say whether they acted rightly or not in any trying situation, which in real life is held in check by a sense of having no business to judge, and of not knowing all the ins and outs of the affair. But as, where fiction is concerned, there is no such restraint, one of the attractions of a good novel whose characters speak and move (as Mrs. Oliphant's always do) like living beings, is the opportunity it gives for the exercise of the aforesaid critical faculty.[2]

The readers who begged Trollope to let Lily Dale marry Johnny Eames, like the mythical critic who counted Lady Macbeth's children, may go directly against the whole bias of modern criticism in favour of the autonomy of art. But their excesses, perhaps, are not much greater than our own, and their reaction does at least reflect what modern formalists often omit, man's valid search in literature for his own image.[3]

Although the concern for character dominated this school of thought, there was also a strong demand for mimetic accuracy in the novel's picturing of facts and events. 'Unnatural situations' is almost as frequent a term of abuse as 'unnatural characters', and the standard is again simply that of external reality. Critics generally rely on their readers' sense of the absurd, making no attempt to examine the credentials of melodrama in fiction, but merely providing a sarcastic paraphrase of the book's events. Conventions like the coincidence and the convenient demise may be acceptable in the theatre, some argue, like

[1] *The Art of Fiction*, p. 22.

[2] lxviii (1892), 648; see also liv (1881), 703–4 (both by 'Miss Dillwyn').

[3] The comprehensiveness of the idea (held by the New Critics and others) that 'character' is merely an abstraction—one dimension of a complex verbal structure, and no more—has been increasingly questioned by a viewpoint that tries to take into account this typical Victorian reaction. John Bayley, for example, has revived the 'sense of life' as a meaningful idea in *The Characters of Love*, 1960. See also Philip Rahv, 'Fiction and the Criticism of Fiction', *Kenyon Rev*. xviii (1956), 276–99.

the *Saturday Review* in 1866, but the novel's essential principle is its closer relation to reality: 'The condition of really enjoying a novel is that we should have a kind of provisional belief in its historical truth; the very purpose of all the little details of conversation and manners is to produce such a temporary illusion. Now, to compose a really neat plot, it is usually considered necessary to make free use of those coincidences which more than anything shock our belief.'[1] As a result, critics are always at their most scathing when they discover a factual error. Detailed verisimilitude is demanded, and any offences against it are considered fatal to the work: reviews abound with triumphant discoveries of minute inaccuracies. It is partly in response to this that George Eliot, for example, makes exhaustive enquiries of Frederic Harrison about legal points in the plot of *Felix Holt*,[2] and Wilkie Collins is upset when he learns, through a *Times* review, of an inconsistency in the arrival-time of a train in *The Woman in White*.[3] Charles Reade's Zolaesque *passion du document* is an exaggerated form, but it represents a genuine doctrine of verification widely observed among novelists of the time.[4]

Another rule follows naturally: that of authorial experience. And like so many others at this level of criticism, it arises out of a valid requirement, but is desperately in need of modification. Besant gives it pride of place among the laws of fiction: 'First, and before everything else, there is the Rule that everything in Fiction which is invented and is not the result of personal experience and observation is worthless.'[5] Or, in the words of Matthew Arnold: '. . . in the novel one prefers, I think, to have the novelist dealing with the life which he knows from having

[1] 'French Novels', xxi (1866), 615–16.

[2] *George Eliot Letters*, iv, 215 ff.

[3] N. P. Davis, *The Life of Wilkie Collins*, Urbana, 1956, pp. 221–2.

[4] See Léone Rives, *Charles Reade, sa vie, ses romans*, Toulouse, 1940, pp. 189–97; and W. C. Phillips, *Dickens, Reade, and Collins: Sensation Novelists*, New York, 1919, pp. 137–9.

[5] *The Art of Fiction*, pp. 15–16. A typical earlier example is in the *Saturday Rev.* xxv (1868), 796–7.

lived it, rather than with the life which he knows from books or hearsay.' Hence, *Anna Karenina* is preferred to *War and Peace*, and *Vanity Fair* to *The Virginians*.[1] Often, the rule is applied to damn quite justifiably an ignorant or careless writer. But the real ramifications of the problem—the various *kinds* of 'experience'—are ignored, and the demand for it is significant simply as another facet of the general demand for realism.

It is surprising that out of such a strong and perpetual tendency in criticism a more detailed theory of outright realism did not arise. One early champion of naturalism, however, does present some interesting ideas: an anonymous reviewer of William Gilbert's *De Profundis*, in the *Spectator* for 1865. Gilbert is matched only by Defoe, according to the writer, for his presentation of the very ore of life, free from all the processes of modification by which other novelists produce a clear '*intellectual* picture'. The 'delusive sense of solid fact' is achieved by a piling-up of detail, apparently quarried out of the narrator's memory rather than refined for us by his imagination. The effect on the reader is that of the raw material of experience itself, out of the mass of which different writers could still evolve three or four different stories. Yet such writing is nevertheless a product of the writer's imagination: Gilbert succeeds 'not because he has strung together details instead of imagined them, but because he has imagined events in their natural detail'. All authorial interpretation is eschewed, as is the 'falsifying' effect of association when events are described by the characters themselves:

The true difference between such stories as these and ordinary novels is that novelists usually aim at painting the *expression* of character, while this class of stories represent not its expression, but its influence as an active cause upon the circumstances of life, and their reaction upon it. No less imagination is required for the one task than the other, but it is the imagination of an interpreting mind in the one case, and of an acting will in the other. The intellectual novelist tries to think of what is most expressive of a particular state of mind;

[1] 'Count Leo Tolstoi', *Fortnightly Rev.* xlii, n.s. (1887), 784–5.

De Foe and his school only of what a man would actually *do* under certain circumstances, and not at all what that doing might mean. The one school treats motive as a secret constituent of character, to be brought into the picture as a feature of interest,—the other does not analyse motive at all, but simply presses on to the resulting action leaving its probable complexity of various motives unsifted. But imagination of the most tenacious kind is not less necessary, probably more necessary, to work out actions than to display character.[1]

Such accounts are rare, however, and it remains true that criticism based on total realism is almost always superficial—though at the same time ubiquitous. The significance of the tendency should neither be overlooked nor exaggerated. When Trollope, as novelist and theorist, is called typical of his age and race, there is a measure of justice in the assertion. But when one modern critic picks out only those Victorian concepts of fiction based on 'Truthfulness with regard to facts and truthfulness with regard to character', and dismisses all others as the unimportant (and neo-Fascist) detritus of Romanticism, then justice disappears.[2] Truth-to-life dominated the naïve approach, and, much qualified, influenced others on a higher plane; but each admitted qualification, like the bend in a mirror, altered the truthful image, and made the idea of simple realism the less tenable.

II. PLEASING IMAGES

The first modification in the glass is almost as ancient as the theory of imitation itself. Basically, its origins lie in the Horatian tenet that art is a pleasure-giving activity, and, even more generally, in the traditional aesthetic principle of audience-effect which Meyer Abrams calls 'the principal aesthetic attitude of the Western world'.[3] As far as poetic theory was concerned, attention had largely shifted by the end of the eighteenth

[1] xxxviii (1865), 71–73. Dr. R. H. Tener of the University of Alberta attributes this review, on internal evidence, to R. H. Hutton.

[2] Frank O'Connor, *The Mirror in the Roadway*, London, 1957, p. 10.

[3] *The Mirror and the Lamp*, New York, 1953, p. 21.

century from audience to artist; but the change was much less evident in the criticism of fiction. Even though the actual comments made on the novel are often individually trivial, it is the widespread assumptions behind them which add up to this fact of literary history. Implicit in them all is the recognition that mimesis must bow to a higher law, that the purpose of the novel is to give pleasure, and that the novelist must select his material, or transmute it, with this in mind.

The straightforward realism of Trollope arouses a surprising amount of disparagement along these lines—surprising, that is, if it is imagined that the whole age was Trollopean. *London Society*, for example, in 1869, laments his inability to transform prosaic subject-matter, and compares the pleasure of mere recognition derived from his pictures to that of wearing an old pair of slippers.[1] The *Athenaeum*, often depreciatory about Trollope, finds *Phineas Redux* in 1874 thoroughly lifelike, but unideal and depressing[2]; while for the *Spectator* in 1878 *The American Senator* is, like all his recent books, no more than 'leaves from the lives of respectable people'.[3] Finally, in 1901 Leslie Stephen notes the dullness of Trollope's method: 'By the excision of all that is energetic, or eccentric, or impulsive, or romantic, you do not really become more lifelike; you only limit yourself to the common and uninteresting.'[4] Still active behind much of this is the old neo-classic stratagem of judging a work of art according to its high or low subject-matter. Like Matthew Arnold commending 'great actions' and Walter Bagehot criticizing the grotesque, the many detractors of Trollope are firmly in this tradition when they express the belief that 'no amount of skill can make common-place men and common-place incidents and common-place feelings fit subjects of high or true literary art'.[5]

[1] 'The Piccadilly Papers', xv (1869), 473–4.

[2] 1874 (i), 53.

[3] li (1878), 1101–2.

[4] 'Anthony Trollope' (1901), *Studies of a Biographer*, Second Series, 1902, iv, 201.

[5] J. Herbert Stack, 'Mr. Anthony Trollope's Novels', *Fortnightly Rev.* v, n.s. (1869), 196–7.

In the last two decades of the century the theory that what is unpleasant or ugly in life must remain so in art, and consequently must be shunned by novelists, comes inevitably in conflict with the 'slum school' of Moore, Gissing, Arthur Morrison, Richard Whiteing, and others. '. . . When this conscientious realist makes the inebriated Sarah Tucker vomit outside the Criterion, the reader is almost fain to follow her example', objects *The Times* to Moore's *Esther Waters* in 1894[1]; and the earlier *A Mummer's Wife* is disapproved of by the *Athenaeum* and the *Spectator* not for being immoral, but simply for being realistic to an unpleasant and boring degree.[2] Ian Maclaren, despairing over the new realism in 1897, wishes to exclude all ugliness from art as an offence against its principle of offering consolation and recreation: 'It is the substance not the workmanship which offends and repels. . . . One breathes throughout an atmosphere of filth, squalor, profanity, and indecency, and is seized with moral nausea. There are such things as drains, and sometimes they may have to be opened, but one would not for choice have one opened in his library.'[3] The idea is often expressed in terms of the delicate palate: to the end of the century one of the commonest requirements of reviewers is that the novel's realism be limited by the necessity of producing 'a pleasant taste'. The *Edinburgh Review*, for example, formulates the principle in 1896: 'We believe that the surest test of a good novel is that it leaves a pleasant flavour behind'—and goes on to gather its own favourite nosegay at the bottom of the Scottish Kailyard.[4]

The limiting factor is commonly one of social class: the aesthetic response of an élite. Thus, the *Athenaeum* in 1865 warns its readers that in William Gilbert's works they will find themselves in unrelieved association with the unwashed: 'The social world displayed is not congenial to the habits and feelings of cultivated people. . . . No workmanship can make base

[1] 15 May 1894, p. 10.
[2] *Athenaeum*, 1884 (ii), 767; *Spectator*, lviii (1885), 83–85 (by J. A. Noble).
[3] 'Ugliness in Fiction', *Literature*, i (1897), 80–81.
[4] 'The New Scottish Novelists', clxxxiv (1896), 38 (by A. Innes Shand).

material worthy to endure for any length of time, nor make it capable of being formed into "a vessel of honour".'[1] And H. H. Lancaster, writing on George Eliot in 1866, points out, as do so many, that lower-class characters by virtue of their position in life can never evoke that sympathy which sets off tragedy from the merely harrowing.[2] It is as if the social idealism of snobbery has become an aesthetic idealism and a principle of artistic selection.

The widespread demand that art should be pleasing before it is realistic can also be traced with regard to two distinct conventions in the novel: the 'agreeable' character and the happy ending. Both of these are frequently praised or accepted by critics as natural features of the world of fiction, though they are rarely recognized as being as much a distortion of reality as the devices of melodrama which so many of the same critics deplored. In these two conventions, the reader was able to find the Meliorist ideas of the hopefulness and coherence of the universe which the Victorians sought, and which were so often denied to them in the plain renderings of the realists.

The first is one of the most familiar clichés in reviewing. For many critics, it is almost as reprehensible for the figures of a novel to be unpleasant people as it is for them to be 'unnatural'. Both criteria are used side by side, without any apparent sense of contradiction: for example, the hero and heroine of Holme Lee's *Basil Godfrey's Caprice* are praised as being natural, and at the same time as having been made pleasing and perfect by a process of idealization that shows a true conception of art.[3] 'Natural' proves to be a fairly complex term, involving not only factual closeness to life and convincingness within the structure of the novel, but also the distinction that what seems most natural in art, as in life, is life's happier side. When Saintsbury complains, of Florence Marryat's *How They Loved Him*, that the

[1] 1865 (i), 124.

[2] 'George Eliot's Novels', *North British Rev.* vi, n.s. (1866), 207. J. Herbert Stack, in the article quoted above, makes the same point about Hetty Poyser in *Adam Bede* ('Mr. Anthony Trollope's Novels', *Fortnightly Rev.* v, n.s., 1869, 191).

[3] *British Quarterly Rev.* xlvii (1868), 553–4.

characters are all contemptible, and that 'A man of Sir Gilbert Conroy's class does not shake his wife when he learns that she was unfit to be his wife', he is not just criticizing a lack of correspondence with the normal facts of life (although that is important in his eyes), but is also implying that fiction should portray a world where people and behaviour are to a large extent stylized in order to reassure. He goes on:

To say of a book that it is disagreeable is sometimes thought to be a feeble, not to say feminine, form of criticism. In truth, it is nothing of the kind, but (if the word is used in its proper sense) one of the severest and most final reprobations possible of any product of art. A book may be as pitiful or terrible as its author can make it (they are not often able to make it either, more's the pity), but if it is disagreeable it is bad.[1]

Without at least some agreeable figures in a story, it is felt that a writer cannot establish the essential rapport with his readers, as when C. L. Graves is repelled by Stevenson's *The Master of Ballantrae*: 'One feels the want of a congenial character amongst the *dramatis personae* on whom one's sympathies can be legitimately bestowed.'[2] And the same reviewer makes a revealing criticism of a passage in Gissing's *The Crown of Life* (Chapter 14) which begins: 'He arrived at his hotel in London late at night, drank a glass of spirits, and went to bed. . . .' After a longer quotation, Graves concludes firmly: 'That is finely said, and yet the impression is seriously impaired by that detestable and gratuitous touch of realism at the outset about the glass of spirits. In his perfect but inartistic sincerity, Mr. Gissing insists on playing the valet to his hero, with the result of destroying any sentimental attachment on the part of the reader.'[3] There is more to this than an abstainer's disapproval of spirits. The insistence that the central character must be a degree above life can be seen as a reversion to yet another of the ideas of neo-classicism.

[1] *Academy*, xxii (1882), 45. See also his criticism of Thackeray's *Philip* in 1908 (*A Consideration of Thackeray*, 1931, p. 243).

[2] *Spectator*, lxiii (1889), 437–8.

[3] ibid. lxxxiii (1899), 661–2.

The happy ending receives less explicit comment, and can be considered a critical principle more by its tacit acceptance than by its open recommendation. The *Dublin University Magazine* in 1865 is fairly representative in its praise of *Sedgely Court* for ending in the marrying-off of amiable characters: 'Sedgely Court is festooned with enduring orange blossom. It is the very type of what should be the principal scene in a novel—a paradise of lovers—a soil where affairs of the heart never failed of fruit.'[1] And R. D. Blackmore enunciates the principle, at the end of *Cradock Nowell*, that the conclusion to a novel should be like the will of a good-natured man, in which tokens of regard and grateful mentions are bestowed on all the author's friends and dependents.[2] Burne-Jones, finally, is a typical reader of this sort in his complaint against *Anna Karenina*: '. . . I can't bear a tale that has in it a woman who is knocked about and made miserable and mad, and thrown away on a wretch, and is altogether heart-breaking. I like such a one, after due troublesomeness and quite bearable anxiety, to marry the hero and be happy ever after.'[3] Serious writers in the later years may argue that the darkness and confusion of reality should be reproduced in the novel; but the distrust of tragedy still remains. So long as it is not an obvious absurdity, the majority even of intelligent critics seem to prefer the conclusion which savours of a happier world than this, or at least one in which the death-bed can be accepted for a sense of 'fulfilment' that gives it a tearful happiness of its own.

Finally, any account of the conflict between the principles of realism and of enjoyment in Victorian taste should include a simple reminder that many novels of the most obvious improbability found a wide approval throughout the period. Despite the readiness to pounce on unnatural incidents, the pleasure-principle allowed a notable amount of praise for the wildest fantasies of

[1] 'A Group of New Novels', lxv (1865), 342.

[2] Revised edn., 1873, p. 459.

[3] Quoted in Lady Georgiana Burne-Jones, *Memorials of Edward Burne-Jones*, 1904, ii, 164.

Rhoda Broughton, Henry Kingsley, Mortimer Collins, Dumas, Hugo, and many other favourites. Even Ouida receives her share of tributes from the most respectable of sources. The *Contemporary* thanks her in 1869 for transporting us into regions fairer and more intense than the 'every-day pettinesses' of fashionable realism[1]; and the *Spectator* enthuses over her *Pascarèl* in 1873 for the very fact that it is preposterous, wild, luscious, and beautiful, without any 'touch of realism, of possibility' to spoil its poetry and its fascinating excess.[2] Naturally, there is often disparagement mixed with the praise, to the effect that this kind of fiction, while perfectly valid, is of a lower order than that based on observation and realism. But the existence cannot be ignored of a well-accredited school of thought which accepts the artist's right to transcend nature in his desire to please and entertain: an aim that can result in fairy-tale and romance as well as the avoidance of the trivial, the pessimistic, and the disagreeably real.

III. THE SUBJECTIVE ARTIST

There were no Coleridges among reviewers of the novel; but many of them do pay attention to the effects of the novelist's imagination on the world he portrays. To link this imagination with out-and-out naturalism, as in the *Spectator* review of William Gilbert,[3] is rare; and normally, it is seen as an opponent of mimesis, a power *over* the world of ordinary reality, forcing it into strange and wonderful shapes that impel acceptance. G. H. Lewes in 1872, seeking to explain the difference between Dickens's popularity and his low reputation among the cognoscenti, suggests the very force of his imagination, by which totally false characters affect the reader with a sense of reality and a vividness bordering on that of hallucination. But Lewes has little time for the free play of such a distorting faculty as Dickens's, and he ends by belittling those who are taken in by

[1] x (1869), 315–17. [2] xlvi (1873), 409–10. [3] See above, pp. 27–28.

it.[1] Greater confidence in the imagination—and in Dickens—is shown by Robert Buchanan and Alfred Austin, the first of whom, in a whimsical article in 1872, praises the novelist as a poet and magician, 'to be bound by none of your commonplace laws and regular notions', while Austin, two years before, sees the key to Dickens's greatness in his transcendence of reality through his power of Vision.[2] All three are contradicted by George Stott, whose criticism of Dickens in the *Contemporary* for 1869 is that he lacked true imagination: his idealized fairy-land is really based on the eye, resulting merely in the external and the grotesque rather than the thoughtful exploration below the surface of reality which is the real mark of the imaginative artist.[3]

There are always critics, at all parts of the period, who express a preference for some such subjectivity of treatment. Following Schiller, the *Westminster* in 1867 defines the perfect novel as one 'where incident shall be reconciled with the subjective spirit'[4]; and six years later it condemns the productions of its own age of drab realism: 'Our painting is mere photography, and our descriptive writing is mere topography. Mind is not seen. The play and grace of imagination are lost.'[5] Arthur Symons in the following decade finds the quality exemplified in Meredith, who gives us true creation, instead of mere reporting, through 'the imaginative fusion of the mass of observed fact'.[6] And in 1899 he finds the same in the figure of Balzac, 'a poet whose dreams were facts' and who achieved that effect of all great artists, the near-apotheosis of his characters through the force of his own creative imagination.[7]

[1] 'Dickens in Relation to Criticism', *Fortnightly Rev.* xi, n.s. (1872), 144–9. For a fuller study of Lewes, see M. Greenhut, 'George Henry Lewes as a Critic of the Novel', *Studies in Philology*, xlv (1948), 491–511; and Richard Stang, op. cit. pp. 79–86, 171–6.

[2] Robert Buchanan, 'The "Good Genie" of Fiction', *Saint Paul's*, x (1872), 130–48; Alfred Austin, 'Charles Dickens', *Temple Bar*, xxix (1870), 561–2.

[3] 'Charles Dickens', x (1869), 210–13.

[4] xxxi, n.s. (1867), 261.

[5] xliv, n.s. (1873), 254.

[6] *Time*, i, n.s. (1885), 633.

[7] 'Balzac', *Fortnightly Rev.* lxv, n.s. (1899), 745–57.

Two enthusiastic descriptions of how this divine afflatus of the artist works are given in the *British Quarterly* and the *Gentleman's Magazine*. The former, in the rapturous account of Meredith already quoted, distinguishes the creators from the mere constructors of novels by this subjectivity that assimilates all things to itself and 'achieves its loftiest triumph in so moulding all conceivable relations, be they natural or supernatural, fact or dream, into the ideal form of their own all-fusing imagination, that they issue before us at once as though created by that inner fire, yet as wholly true to the essential laws of human life, and recognized by us as nature itself'.[1] And Garnet Smith, in the *Gentleman's*, arrives at a similar estimate of the true artistic balance that only the creative mind can achieve: 'Our will is free, our character is beautiful, in proportion as they rise above nature. Nature is the material which must pass through the alembic of man's mind; a series of symbols whereby to express the workings of the human soul; the brute matter which owes all its form to art. Yet art, Antaeus-like, is ever reinvigorated by touching mother-earth; and both elements are truly requisite.'[2] Most criticisms based on the nature of the artist's imagination end, in this way, by trying to maintain a balance between the claims of realism and idealism. The imagination is rarely allowed a free rein, and excessive subjectivity is often frowned upon: Turgenev, for example, a great favourite of the Victorians, is almost as frequently commended for controlling his poetic imagination by his accuracy to nature as he is for avoiding naturalism.[3]

By the nineties the reaction against French theories of impersonality in art had given further stimulus to the advocates of subjectivity. For Hubert Crackanthorpe, himself a supposed disciple of Maupassant, all art is imaginative, 'seen through the temperament of a single man', and realism and idealism are

[1] 'The Novels of George Meredith, lxix (1879), 413–14 (by Arabella Shore). See above, p. 8.

[2] 'Gustave Flaubert', cclxv (1888), 120–31.

[3] e.g. *Academy*, xxiv (1883), 179–80.

mutually dependent. The dichotomy does not exist for the artist, for whom simply 'the essential is contained in the frank, fearless acceptance . . . of his entire artistic temperament, with its qualities and its flaws'.[1] And similarly, Gissing, for all his indebtedness to French and Russian naturalism, and for all his early ideas on his own objectivity,[2] comes to define realism as 'nothing more than artistic sincerity in the portrayal of contemporary life'. All material is dead until the writer's imagination and soul have breathed life into it: '. . . what can be more absurd than to talk about the "objectivity" of such an author as Flaubert, who triumphs by his extraordinary power of presenting life as he, and no other man, beheld it? There is no science of fiction.'[3]

In particular, 'sympathy' is singled out as a quality of temperament essential to the artistic shaping of experience, and its lack is often named as the greatest single fault of the French realists. The *Spectator*, for example, condemns the 'clear, correct, and dreary record' of Maupassant's *Fort Comme la Mort* in 1889 as 'totally lacking the one essential element, the *raison d'être* of all Art,—human sympathy'.[4] The English are held up, in comparison, as examples of the power of authorial sympathy—Garnet Smith attributes it to the latent religious feeling in the English mind[5]—and, at times, the Russians, among whom even Dostoesvsky is praised for the sense of personal compassion with which he enfolds his repulsive subject-matter.[6] The subjective element which these critics demand is essentially more than a mere colouring of sentiment. It can imply the whole involvement of the artist in his creation, and it leads to what Vernon Lee, for one, saw as the heart of the ultimate mystery

[1] 'Reticence in Literature. Some Roundabout Remarks', *Yellow Book*, ii (1894), 261, 269.

[2] e.g. *Letters of George Gissing to Members of his Family*, ed. A. and E. Gissing, 1927, pp. 128–9.

[3] 'The Place of Realism in Fiction', *Humanitarian*, New York, vii (1895), 14–16.

[4] lxiii (1889), 309–10.

[5] 'Gustave Flaubert', *Gentleman's Mag.* cclxv (1888), 130.

[6] e.g. 'Dostoiefski', *Temple Bar*, xci (1891), 249.

of aesthetics: that 'un-real truthfulness' which subdues our soul, and can only be called the author's '*sympathy*, or passionate personal interest'.[1]

IV. HIGHER REALMS

Even more clearly anti-realist than any of the tendencies we have yet seen is that which describes the novelist's goal in transcendental terms, such as Beauty, or Truth, or Essence—words implying the familiar concept of an ideal world beyond the phenomena of life, but accessible to art. A. Eubule-Evans, for example, in *St. Paul's* for 1873, describes the novelist as penetrating to a realm of the True and the Beautiful through reproducing Nature in its broad, rather than its detailed, features. A lesson is to be taken from the works of the Germans, Spielhagen and Auerbach, who aim not at externals but at Essence itself.[2] Mrs. Oliphant finds her exemplars for this effect in Charles Reade and Lord Lytton, both of whom scorn mere vulgar reproduction, and aim always at 'a lofty soul under the garments of individual existence' and at a reality best represented by 'dreams truer than the facts'.[3] And in 1885 W. E. Henley uses *Diana of the Crossways* to enunciate a doctrine that would hardly have sounded strange on the lips of Johnson or Sir Joshua Reynolds: 'This is indeed the merit and distinction of art: to be more real than reality, to be not nature, but nature's essence. It is the artist's function not to copy, but to synthesize; to eliminate from that gross confusion of actuality which is his raw material whatever is accidental, idle, irrelevant, and select for perpetuation that only which is appropriate and immortal.'[4]

An idealist theory of fiction along these lines is Thomas Hardy's: in fact, his eventual abandonment of the novel for

[1] 'Rosny and the French Analytical Novel', *Cosmopolis*, vii (1897), 690–1.

[2] 'German Novelists', xii (1873), 277–89.

[3] 'Charles Reade's Novels', *Blackwood's Edinburgh Mag.* cvi (1869), 514; 'Lord Lytton', ibid. cxiii (1873), 376.

[4] *Athenaeum*, 1885 (i), 339-40.

poetry can perhaps be foreseen in the high, Sidneyan aims he set for it. In spite of his insistence on verisimilitude—as seen in the rigorous time-charts, topographies, and biographies of characters he always drew up for his novels, as well as his qualified approval for the naturalists' revolution against the artificial—fiction remained for him, like all art, something higher than life, 'more true, so to put it, than nature or history can be'. The modern school of 'novelists of social minutiae', with their 'photographic curiousness', present only 'life garniture and not life'.[1] Hardy continually emphasizes the transcendental ends of art, writing in his notebook in 1890: 'Art is a disproportioning—(*i.e.* distorting, throwing out of proportion)—of realities, to show more clearly the features that matter in those realities, which, if merely copied or reported inventorially, might possibly be observed, but would more probably be overlooked. Hence "realism" is not Art.' In 1877 he describes the novel as, like poetry, a mode of discovery, which makes the defects of nature 'the basis of a hitherto unperceived beauty, by irradiating them with "the light that never was" on their surface, but is seen to be latent in them by the spiritual eye'. And in 1886, as *The Mayor of Casterbridge* was appearing: 'My art is to intensify the expression of things, as is done by Crivelli, Bellini, etc., so that the heart and inner meaning is made vividly visible.'[2] External perception is the foundation, but the true novelist must always lead us into a new world by his transforming faculties: 'A sight for the finer qualities of existence, an ear for the "still sad music of humanity".'[3] From such idealist statements as these, a modern study of Hardy as a theorist concludes that in

[1] 'The Profitable Reading of Fiction', *Forum*, New York, v (1888), 63–65. The general critical reaction to Hardy reflected this dualism in his theory, critics never being sure by which standard, realist or non-realist, to appraise his stylized characters and incidents. See W. J. Hyde, 'Hardy's View of Realism: a Key to the Rustic Characters', *Victorian Studies*, ii (1958–9), 45–59.

[2] Quoted in F. E. Hardy, *The Early Life of Thomas Hardy*, 1928, pp. 299, 150–1, 231–2.

[3] 'The Science of Fiction', *New Rev.* iv (1891), 315–19.

his criticism (as in his novels) he belongs to the tradition of Melville, Emily Brontë, and Hawthorne: 'He now appears to us as a realist developing towards allegory—as an imaginative artist who brought the nineteenth-century novel out of its slavery to fact.'[1]

One aspect of the idealist author's quest for the universal is his use of type-characters. On the whole, these are not popular with reviewers, as offending against the dominant principle of lifelikeness, but it is not at all uncommon to find such perfectly neo-classic accounts as that of Mowbray Morris in 1882: 'The fictions which paint the manners and humours of contemporary life, which deal with portraits rather than with types of humanity, with the individualities of nature rather, and not with her universal and eternal properties, must inevitably lose . . . much of that which once constituted its chiefest charm.'[2] Often, a compromise is the solution, and many critics praise figures in fiction which somehow transcend the realistic or the particularized yet maintain their roots in the everyday (the compromise, for that matter, is also neo-classic). Saintsbury, for example, sees the type as something that emerges from a strongly individualized character, criticizing Feuillet for his failure to achieve this.[3] And H. G. Wells, in the *Saturday Review*, holds up Turgenev as an example of that 'highest form of literary art' by which a character is made typical *and* individual at the same time, a living figure lit through with symbolism—in this case (typically with Wells), the symbolism of great forces working in society.[4]

This concept of the symbol—an image from some world of universals—is applied by a number of critics in the later years,

[1] M. D. Zabel, 'Hardy in Defense of his Art: the Aesthetic of Incongruity', *Southern Rev.* vi (1940), 148. An idealist credo, similar in many respects to Hardy's, appears in 1897 from one of his great successors in this task of emancipation—Conrad's Preface to *The Nigger of the 'Narcissus'*.

[2] 'Charles Dickens', *Fortnightly Rev.* xxxii, n.s. (1882), 769.

[3] 'Octave Feuillet', ibid. xxiv, n.s. (1878), 117.

[4] lxxxi (1896), 23–24 (identified in *Edwardians and Late Victorians*, ed. R. Ellmann, New York, 1960, p. 114).

though without elaboration. Oscar Wilde, in 'The Soul of Man Under Socialism', enlists Meredith beneath the banner of the anti-realists in these terms: 'His people not merely live, but they live in thought. One can see them from myriad points of view. They are suggestive. There is soul in them and around them. They are interpretative and symbolic.'[1] George Gissing is more explicit, and ahead of his time, in his discussions of Dickens's social, philosophical, and ethical symbols in his introductions to the Rochester Edition of 1900–1,[2] and in defending the death of Little Nell for its symbolism of the death of innocence in the earlier *Charles Dickens* (1898).[3] But as evidence of his lack of confidence in the approach, he ends the latter book with the contradictory claim that the representative quality of Hugo's characters makes him something other than a novelist: '*Les Misérables* is not rightly to be called a novel; it belongs to the region of symbolic art.' [4]

George Moore, too, uses the word occasionally to emphasize the non-mimetic nature of the novelist's world, as in his admiration of the fixed, symbolic attitudes given by Flaubert to the characters of Frédéric and Arnoux in *L'Éducation Sentimentale*.[5] For Moore, this other world can take the form of the 'under life', a transcendentalized version of the unconscious. He praises Tolstoi, whose actual events are but

> signs and symbols, and the beauty of Tolstoi's art is that nowhere can we determine the limits of either life; so beautifully are they interwoven that they are in the book as they are in life, indivisible forms of one and the same thing. The subconscious is the real life, out of which chance has beckoned us for a while; it is the life of the ages, and through it Tolstoi enables us to perceive affinities in all things.[6]

Lastly, Arthur Symons's *The Symbolist Movement in Literature* draws together many of these anti-naturalist themes in its

[1] *Fortnightly Rev.* xlix, n.s. (1891), 312–13.

[2] Reprinted as *Critical Studies of the Works of Charles Dickens*, New York, 1924.

[3] pp. 176–7.

[4] p. 220.

[5] 'A Tragic Novel', *Cosmopolis*, vii (1897), 52.

[6] 'Since the Elizabethans', ibid. iv (1896), 57.

definition of symbol as 'a representation which does not aim at being a reproduction', and 'some embodiment and revelation of the Infinite; the Infinite is made to blend itself with the Finite'. The novel is now moving away from the mere exteriority and formalism of Flaubert, Zola, and the Goncourts, and by the use of symbol is attaining to 'ultimate essence' and 'the soul of things'. Taking Huysmans as his example, and in language strongly resembling Moore's, Symons shows how the novelist uses detail only in order to symbolize the 'invisible life' which underlies the universe:

Here, then, purged of the distraction of incident, liberated from the bondage of a too realistic conversation, in which the aim had been to convey the very gesture of breathing life, internalised to a complete liberty, in which, just because it is so absolutely free, art is able to accept, without limiting itself, the expressive medium of a convention, we have in the novel a new form, which may be at once a confession and a decoration, the soul and a pattern.[1]

Of the various kinds of *belle nature* which fiction might strive to represent, there remains that of the 'Aesthetic' dream, the independent world of 'pure' beauty itself—a concept which found short shrift from most novel-critics. Vernon Lee, whose Pateresque 'The Value of the Ideal' stands out incongruously in the sound Tory pages of the *National Review*, defines this beauty largely in terms of the 'aesthetic sense' of readers, which is left ungratified by the mere factuality of a Zola.[2] But a more objective world of beauty for the novel is celebrated in Oscar Wilde's famous 'The Decay of Lying' in 1889, a brilliant piece of exaggeration and rhetoric, with just enough implication of sense to prevent it taking off on the wings of its own exuberance. Lying, he insists, is the basis of true art, which has now been debased into a mere blue-book by the drabness and insignificance of contemporary realism, Meredith being one of the few who has 'refused to bow the knee to Baal' and kept 'life at a respectful distance'. Art is dragged down by the contemporary, since beauty cannot exist in things to which we are not

[1] 1899, pp. 3–10, 141–50. [2] vi (1885–6), 26–42.

indifferent, as witness the tragic decline of Reade from the beauty of *The Cloister and the Hearth* to his later social polemic: 'Certainly we are a degraded race, and have sold our birthright for a mess of facts.'

Wilde then establishes his main point, that art is independent of reality and of life—'poor, probable, uninteresting human life' —and the key to its existence is beauty alone. After a grotesque vision of the world of dragons and basilisks that would succeed a revival of lying, he summarizes the doctrines that are to guide prose-writer and poet:

> All bad art comes from returning to life and nature, and elevating them into ideals. Life and nature may sometimes be used as part of art's rough material, but before they are of any real service to art they must be translated into artistic conventions. The moment art surrenders its imaginative medium it surrenders everything. As a method Realism is a complete failure, and the two things that every artist should avoid are modernity of form and modernity of subject-matter.

Life imitates art, and can only express its energy through art; and lastly, lying is the aim of art, 'the telling of beautiful untrue things'.[1]

For all the witty extravagance of Wilde's argument, it is a contribution of some significance in the discussion of the novel's relation to real life. Idealism has reached its flood-mark in his creation of a wholly independent world for the novel to embody, a world of beauty which can be defined only in terms of itself. Never was the mirror more distorted, and never was mimesis more splendidly routed.

V. A WORLD OF ILLUSION

Other critics of fiction, less concerned with transcendental matters, discuss the problem of illusion within the novel itself—the 'sense of reality' that is produced more by its inner coherence than by its correspondence with the normal or the ideal

[1] *Nineteenth Century*, xxv (1889), 35–56.

world. Defoe is often recognized as a key-figure in this respect, and in 1868 Leslie Stephen, for example, follows the traditional pattern of admiring his sleight-of-hand, the ingenious presentation of corroborative evidence by apparently impartial witnesses, and the warnings against believing too completely in his characters, by which this writer wins conviction.[1] However, Stephen places little value on 'the mere fact of producing a truthful narrative', and elsewhere in the same issue of the *Cornhill* he comes down heavily against the whole idea of illusion in fiction. He defends Richardson's device of narration by letters, and dismisses its improbability as irrelevant:

It is not the object of a really good novelist, nor does it come within the legitimate means of high art in any department, to produce an actual illusion . . . a novelist is not only justified in writing so as to prove that his work is fictitious; but he almost necessarily hampers himself, to the prejudice of his work, if he imposes upon himself the condition that his book shall be capable of being mistaken for a genuine narrative.[2]

Stephen repeats his point in 1877, disparaging the illusive realism of Defoe, and also criticizing the character of Paul Emanuel, in *Villette*, as *too* real, a product of the 'erroneous theory of art' that literature aims simply at illusion.[3]

Stephen's depreciative use of the word 'illusion' is misleading. What he is attacking is the school of thought which believed that aesthetic acceptance can only be secured in the reader by directly imitative means. He is not rejecting the effect of acceptance itself, which can, of course, result from the most stylized manipulation of reality. In fact, it is precisely this effect that he praises as arising from Richardson's non-realism, in the 1868 article: 'There is, indeed, no reason for looking closely; so long as the situations bring out the desired sentiment, we may accept them for the nonce, without asking whether they could possibly

[1] 'De Foe's Novels', *Cornhill Mag.* xvii (1868), 294–8.

[2] 'Richardson's Novels', ibid. p. 54.

[3] 'Hours in a Library. XVII.—Charlotte Brontë', ibid. xxxvi (1877), 727, 733.

have occurred.'[1] 'Desired sentiment', it appears from the context, is simply the particular conviction or illusion, in the wider sense of the word, at which the author is aiming, and towards which he is using the fictional techniques at his disposal.

The issue is plainly the Aristotelian one of the likely impossibility against the unconvincing possibility. Mrs. Oliphant, for example, criticizes certain improbabilities in the novels of Charles Reade: 'Such a thing might happen in fact; but fiction is bound as fact is not.' Anything at all can happen in life, but 'fiction is bound by harder laws than fact is, and must consider *vraisemblance* as well as absolute truth'.[2] And the *Westminster Review* in 1866 is not reconciled by Dickens's defence of *Our Mutual Friend* that it is true to life: '. . . how does that affect the matter? Truth is not always probable. And it is probability which is required in a novel.'[3] Some suggest that this *vraisemblance* is achieved neither by the devices of artistic form, nor by plain mimesis, but by *selective* representation of the familiar. The more common the event in real life, the more acceptable does it seem when transposed into an artistic world where the effect of naturalness is always more difficult to achieve, and where every factor in favour of belief must be called into play. For example: 'In real life we accept such facts because they *are* facts; but in reading a novel, the whole groundwork is so necessarily make-believe, that the facts must seem very natural to make us forget their unreality.'[4] And, of one of those railway accidents so topical and so useful for the Victorian novelist: 'Such *coups de théâtre* may happen occasionally in real life, for fact has a wonderful contempt for the balance of events; but everywhere else it offends us. . . . The domain of the novelist is nature under its ordinary rules; not fact, which is often irreconcilable with life. We allow that an accident is possible enough: still it has an undesirable suddenness, and is, however real, an artificial

[1] 'Richardson's Novels', ibid. xvii (1868), 66.

[2] 'Charles Reade's Novels', *Blackwood's Edinburgh Mag.* cvi (1869), 510.

[3] xxix, n.s. (1866), 582–5.

[4] J. Herbert Stack, 'Some Recent English Novels', *Fortnightly Rev.* ix, n.s. (1871), 743.

incident.'[1] For this latter commentator at least, the world of reality, in its moments of aberration, can seem like a bad novel.

However, many others see that probability depends on certain internal conventions which are part of the nature of art. In 1869 Harry Buxton Forman, like Leslie Stephen, accepts the epistolary devices of *Clarissa*, on the grounds that character is never convincing until it has been modified by this, or a similar, convention: 'Art is more piquant in its results than life is by just this power of making all surrounding circumstances subservient to the central idea.'[2] And in the same year another writer asks why the majority opinion of the day, which holds art's business to be faithful reproduction, cannot see that when a novel convinces by its 'naturalness' its artistic method is actually the reverse. Dialogue, for example, and character-drawing are always selective: 'Realism is reached by unreal means; naturalness by artificial aids; simplicity by what may be called the necessary exaggeration of art.'[3] R. L. Stevenson makes a similar complaint about the public to Henry James in 1884: 'They think that striking situations, or good dialogue, are got by studying life; they will not rise to understand that they are prepared by deliberate artifice and set off by painful suppressions.'[4] And the technician's contempt for the idea of character being a Pygmalian miracle comes out again four years later, in his statement that characters 'are only strings of words and parts of books; they dwell in, they belong to, literature; convention, technical artifice, technical gusto, the mechanical necessities of the art, these are the flesh and blood with which they are invested'.[5]

Like Richardson, Dickens is a writer whose obvious reliance on the artificial encourages some critics to examine the nature of illusion. George Stott, for example, in a valuable article in

[1] 'Recent Novels', *Fraser's Mag.* xx, n.s. (1879), 560.

[2] 'Samuel Richardson, as Artist and Moralist', *Fortnightly Rev.* vi, n.s. (1869), 430–1, 442–3.

[3] 'The Exaggeration of Art', *Once a Week*, iii, n.s. (1869), 123–5.

[4] *Letters*, ed. S. Colvin, 1911, ii, 216–17.

[5] 'Some Gentlemen in Fiction', *Scribner's Mag.* New York, iii (1888), 767.

1869, dismisses Pre-Raphaelite ideas about the close reproduction of nature, and criticizes Dickens not for his unreality but for his unimaginative use of the conventions that all art insists upon. An exact copy of life, even if it were possible, would seem unlifelike, and the illusion of life in a novel is secured by 'compression' of facts and 'grouping' of characters.[1]

A partial defence of Dickens, on the grounds of art's conventionality, emerges from the contradictions of Gissing's well-known study at the end of the century. He continually criticizes Dickens's improbable plots and melodramatic devices, yet one side of Gissing is ready to admit that what is effective is thereby artistically justified, and that the rules ought to be re-written to admit it. He attacks the use of coincidences in *Bleak House*, obviously uneasy at Dickens's powers of persuasion:

> Therein lies the worthlessness of the plot, which is held together only by the use of coincidence in its most flagrant forms. Grant that anything may happen just where or when the interest of the story demands it, and a neat drama may pretty easily be constructed. The very boldness of the thing prevents readers from considering it; indeed most readers take the author's own view, and imagine every artificiality to be permitted in the world of fiction.

Yet Gissing goes on to accept that novel's account of the death of Krook by spontaneous combustion, admitting implicitly that events in a novel should be judged within the reader's total reaction to the book, under the spell of this very boldness of the author: 'No doubt the generality of readers are wise, and it is pedantry to object to the logical extremes of convention in an art which, without convention, would not exist.'[2]

Further on in the book, in a general consideration of his author's characters, he again hints at convention being justified

[1] 'Charles Dickens', *Contemporary Rev.* x (1869), 205–10.

[2] *Charles Dickens*, 1898, pp. 57–58. See also his acceptance of coincidences in fiction in a letter of 1891 (*Letters of George Gissing to Eduard Bertz*, ed. A. C. Young, London, 1961, pp. 132–3); and his liking for the conventional as a reason for preferring fiction to the drama ('Why I Don't Write Plays', *Pall Mall Gazette*, lv, 10 September 1892, 3).

by the illusion which it alone can produce. Characters like Mrs. Gamp seem true, yet would be impossible in real life: 'Is not the fact in itself very remarkable, that by dint (it seems) of *omitting* those very features which in life most strongly impress us, an artist in fiction can produce something which we applaud as an inimitable portrait?' Through a subtle idealizing process, of which humour is the chief medium, we arrive at 'a sublimation of the essence of Gamp'. When the process breaks down, Dickens gives us his melodramatic heroines and incredible children—cases where he has meant to exalt fact through the imagination, and has only succeeded in making fact disappear: 'In Mrs. Gamp a portion of truth is omitted; in Alice Marlow there is substitution of falsity. By the former process, true idealism *may* be reached; by the latter, one arrives at nothing but attitude and sham.'

And towards the end, Gissing repeats his earlier words in defending his subject from disparaging comparisons with such realists as Balzac and Daudet. Every writer, he claims, must follow his own mode, and 'realism' must be seen as a merely relative term: 'As soon as a writer sits down to construct a narrative, to imagine human beings, or adapt those he knows to changed circumstances, he enters a world distinct from the actual, and, call himself what he may, he obeys certain laws, certain conventions, without which the art of fiction could not exist.'[1] G. H. Ford, discussing Gissing's interpretation of Dickens, calls him a firm realist who has been forced into mere impressionism when faced by the Master's distortions of reality.[2] But it would be fairer to conclude, from his remarks on Dickens alone, that this was a realist who at times could see and, with hesitations, accept the unreality and autonomy of any novelist's world.

Such a large concept as this, of course, could be detected in areas of criticism outside the actual debate over the *vrai* and the *vraisemblable*. Technical discussions of plot, for example, often

[1] *Charles Dickens*, pp. 88–93, 216–18.

[2] *Dickens and his Readers*, Princeton, 1955, pp. 245–9.

recognize that it is inherently conventional, and when a novelist tries to imitate the confusion of real events, without concentration or arrangement, he is seen to sin against the most basic (and anti-mimetic) of artistic principles, that of formal unity—as does Trollope, according to the *Saturday* in 1869, and Tolstoi, according to Julia Wedgwood in 1887.[1] Characters are all the time required to be, in common reviewers' shorthand, 'grouped', 'balanced', 'worked up', or in other ways artificially arranged—and one can read this, too, as an unconscious refutation of the photographic approach. In fact, *any* recognition that the novel has an aesthetic pattern, or a technique, or, for that matter, a moral mission, is an implicit denial of the theory of simple realism. We have been mainly concerned with more open accounts of the novel's representation of reality; but as the ultimate theoretical question, it underlies every other aspect of criticism.

VI. THE REALIST INVASION

The century's conflicting ideas on realism in fiction can be traced with fresh clarity in several well-defined disputes which fluttered the dovecotes during its last twenty years. Two of these arose round the works of the American and the French realists, another round the revival of the romance. Of the first two, it is perhaps surprising that criticism of the novels of Henry James and W. D. Howells should have been more varied and on the whole more valuable than that devoted to Zola. The French naturalists produced a reaction in which questions of morality predominated, whereas the Americans, while receiving their share of moral denunciation, were less obviously offensive, and could be examined with a more strict regard to aesthetic matters.

Most adverse criticism of James and Howells is aimed at their excessive realism, by critics of varying idealist standpoints; but contradictorily, the opposite undercurrent, in favour of

[1] *Saturday Rev.* xxvii (1869), 751–3; 'Count Leo Tolstoi', *Contemporary Rev.* lii (1887), 252.

truth-to-life, reveals itself behind a number of attacks. The very subtlety and workmanship of James, for example, which nearly all acknowledge, are seen by such critics as part and parcel of his unreality. The *British Quarterly Review*, which makes many commendable efforts to come to grips with the new problems presented by James's tangential relation to real life, reluctantly takes issue with *The Madonna of the Future, and other Tales* in 1880: '. . . the sense of reality is never established. He cannot invest his characters with the flesh-and-blood attributes which lay hold of simple sympathies; and airy, delicate, graceful, and refined as are his creations, they belong to a world of make-believe after all, brought into existence and controlled entirely by the intellect and *conscious* artistic sense of the author.'[1] Similarly, Mrs. Oliphant dislikes *The Princess Casamassima* because it seems manufactured, mere enamel with little of the actual in it[2]; and the *Spectator* prefers the 'good palpable flesh-and-blood' of less artistic writers to the mere outer shell of character it is presented with in *The Tragic Muse*.[3]

Much less frequently, Howells is the object of the same complaint. John Barrow Allen, in the *Academy*, regrets that his skill and ingenuity are vitiated by the failure to create living characters in the tradition of Colonel Newcome, Micawber, Jeanie Deans, and Dugald Dalgetty: 'With Mr. Howells the type is everything, the personalities go for little or nothing.'[4] More usually, the advocates of simple realism praise Howells, especially in his later books. For example, in *A Woman's Reason* 'the characters are all consistent creations, each one thinking, acting and speaking as such people would in real life'[5]; and *Annie Kilburn* is commended for portraying 'recognisable flesh and blood: his people do not elude us, as was their wont in the old days; we know them, and can, as it were, grasp their hands'.[6] Finally, one of the most favourable of all reviews is the *Pall Mall*

[1] lxxi (1880), 234–6.
[2] 'Novels', *Blackwood's Edinburgh Mag.* cxl (1886), 786.
[3] lxv (1890), 409–10 (by J. A. Noble).
[4] xliii (1893), 434–5.
[5] *Westminster Rev.* lxv, n.s. (1884), 273.
[6] *Spectator*, lxii (1889), 371–2 (by J. A. Noble).

Gazette's of *The Rise of Silas Lapham* in 1885, which extols the novelist's 'unique photographic genius' for setting itself against the Philistine and outmoded English preference for the unusual and sensational. Howells's reliance on the complete actuality and possibility of every incident and conversation is hailed as a mark of the novel of the future:

. . . of this tendency towards pure character-painting and ordinary incident, Mr. Howells is the furthest living exponent. . . . The after ages will wonder that we preferred our assassins and our bigamists to the Lady of the Aroostook, just as we ourselves wonder that an age which had Colonel Newcome and Becky Sharpe before its eyes could waste its time on the false, crude, and high-flown romanticism of the first Lord Lytton and his idealistic waxworks.[1]

By far the most numerous critics of the American school, however, are those who accept that it is realistic, and proceed to attack realism on the grounds of the essential dullness and triviality of the material, regardless of treatment. The *London Quarterly* puts the relevant question in a review of *The Aspern Papers* in 1889, when it asks whether a perfectly-wrought imitation of life can be a fine art, irrespective of the intrinsic beauty or interest of the scene described.[2] Most give a very definite answer, *à propos* of James, at any rate—Saintsbury, for example, as early as 1877: 'He has read Balzac, if it be possible, just a little too much; has read him until he has fallen into the one sin of his great master, the tendency to bestow refined dissection and analysis on characters which are not of sufficient intrinsic interest to deserve such treatment.'[3] The point is followed up by W. E. Henley in 1882, who, despite his admiration for James's artistry, regrets that his influence has made the tragic development of character less possible than ten years earlier, 'before the nobodies in life had become somebodies in art'. Lucas Malet's *Mrs. Lorimer* is an example of this influence:

There is not enough of daring and strength; and there is too much of restraint, of discrimination, of the fashionable habit of subtlety and

[1] 'A Great American Novel', xlii (11 September 1885), 5.
[2] lxxi (1888–9), 382–3. [3] *Academy*, xii (1877), 33.

BIRKBECK LIBRARY COLLEGE

refinement and would-be suggestiveness . . . the new American method is excellent as far as it goes, but . . . it really does not go very far. As applied to the commonplace in character and life, it is admirably effective; so that by its operation we can be made to feel momentarily interested in such a human vulgarism as Marcia Hubbard, and to accept, for half-an-hour, such an incarnation of the ephemeral as Daisy Miller as a substitute for Hamlet himself. But, applied to the tragic, its effectiveness ceases, and its capacity is felt to be limited.[1]

In the following year the *Quarterly* describes its boredom at James's 'tea-pot style of conversation',[2] and Arthur Tilley in the *National Review*, though claiming to be an admirer, regrets the persistent failure of James and Howells to follow George Eliot's example of investing the homely and everyday with romance. They have chosen, instead, human motives and situations that are essentially unimportant and incapable of giving real artistic pleasure. True realism must modify its materials by a lightness and cheerfulness of touch that will prevent the work from sinking into dullness and vulgarity, but the Americans have debased, not exalted, the commonplace.[3] This 'true realism' is also defined by Mrs. Humphry Ward, in *Macmillan's* for 1884—this time, like Henley, in terms of that passion and vitality which disappear in the minutiae of the American method, and yet are essential to the fundamentally expansive and passionate English imagination: '. . . realism in one form or another is the *zeitgeist* which will master us all, and realism means the great and the passionate things of life as well as the interesting and the piquant things.'[4]

[1] *Academy*, xxii (1882), 377. Although Henley elsewhere asserts the irrelevance of the artist's choice of material, defending Arthur Morrison's *A Child of the Jago* and emphasizing the importance of form, he nevertheless holds to this basic position that verisimilitude is worthless by itself, and that 'the epic note' of Tolstoi, the 'higher and better sort' of realism, is preferable to 'the toothaches and pimples of experience' in Thackeray's subject-matter. cf. M. U. Schappes, 'William Ernest Henley's Principles of Criticism', *P.M.L.A.* xlvi (1931), 1289–1301; and see below, pp. 93–94.

[2] 'American Novels', clv (1883), 213–20 (by L. J. Jennings).

[3] 'The New School of Fiction', i (1883), 263–5.

[4] 'Recent Fiction in England and France', l (1884), 253–4.

On the whole, Howells once again comes off more lightly than James. By 1890 the *Scots Observer* is noticeably in a minority when it ponderously belabours him for straying 'from the highway of art, from the road that leads by Greek temples and spired mediaeval cities to the purple hills and the bountiful plains of the land of New Romance', and sitting down instead in the desert of realism to 'build sand-houses in the dust-heaps'.[1] For by then J. A. Noble in the *Spectator*, like most others, can point to a 'new' Howells, who has left behind his early period of triviality and has now come to use 'characters and incidents which are attractive apart from their treatment'.[2] And, later, C. L. Graves in the same magazine contrasts him with the inartistic subject-matter of James's *The Awkward Age*: '. . . we never remember to have read a novel in which the disproportion between the ability employed and the worth or attractiveness of the characters was more glaring.' Howells's *Ragged Lady* demonstrates how a similar method can be used to greater effect on ordinary, decent, wholesome people as characters.[3]

Apart from the inherently unpleasing nature of their material, the two Americans also come under fire for their pessimism, especially in their blatant avoidance of the happy ending or a sense of any kind of 'completion'. The *British Quarterly*'s remarks are typical. In *The American*, James's 'strong relentless realism leaves a large amount of failure and continuing unhappiness', and imitates life too closely in its omission of the neat winding-up and the 'happy-ever-after': 'We are no great sticklers for conventionality in novel writing, but a novel is an ideal work of art, and we cannot help thinking that the art is defective in construction which leaves issues so loose and destinies so vague.'[4] Quite uncharacteristic of the time is J. M. Robertson's praise in 1884 for this very lack of happy endings in the earlier Howells: '. . . his faithfulness to an actual life which is full of broken threads and pathetic failures'.[5] The majority of

[1] 'Modern Men. Mr. W. D. Howells', iv (1890), 194–5.

[2] lxiv (1890), 342–3. [3] lxxxii (1899), 647–8. [4] lxx (1879), 268–9.

[5] 'Mr. Howells' Novels', *Westminster Rev.* lxvi, n.s. (1884), 350–1.

critics showed in their reactions to James and Howells, as we have seen them do elsewhere, that they wished the novel to be a consolation for the deficiencies of real life, preferably a happy counterweight to life's sadness, but at least a completion and consummation of some kind. When Arthur Tilley complains that readers feel cheated by the lack of a conclusion, he is not demanding of fiction a banal distribution of orange-blossom and annuities, but the kind of ending, even if tragic, which leaves an aesthetic *and* philosophic sense of symmetry:

> For just as in real life it is this craving which helps to convince so many of us that there is another world, in which the tangled threads of this life will be smoothed out; so in the fictitious life of novels the same craving demands that the smoothing out, or rounding off, call it what you will, shall not be absent. For the creatures of imagination have no future life. Visibly they must realise their heritage of weal or woe.[1]

Loud complaint is also made at the lack of imagination, sympathy, and emotional involvement on the part of the authors. *Temple Bar* is representative in its disapproval of James's over-intellectualization, and the failure of his method to seize hold of the reader. Howells, too, is only half-real through the lack of an emotional spark to make his pictures more than stiff photographs of family groups and 'small-beer chronicles of the soul'.[2] A similar charge frequently levelled against James is one of imaginative and emotional cowardice: for example, in *The Princess Casamassima* he is constantly leading readers up to a 'strong situation', then shirks it, with the result that his characters lose reality and seem mere 'aimless beings'[3]; and in *The Tragic Muse* he is criticized for working round a situation from many sides without ever confronting it, and for making his characters *play* at life.[4]

Occasionally, James receives praise from the opposite point of view, as when the *Athenaeum* in 1896 finds *The Other House*

[1] 'The New School of Fiction', *National Rev.* i (1883), 259–60.
[2] 'The New School of American Fiction', lxx (1884), 383–9.
[3] *Athenaeum*, 1886 (ii), 596–7.
[4] ibid. 1890 (ii), 124.

an improvement on his recent works in the way it touches at 'the heart of life': 'Quiet and restrained as are almost all the scenes, the thing palpitates with the emotion belonging to a work of art that has been cast and fused in one supreme effort.'[1] But this reaction is rare, especially in the nineties, as the reviewer himself indicates; and the *Edinburgh Review*'s survey of the American novel in 1891 is far more typical. It condemns 'the New England school of impersonal realists' for lacking the passion and imaginativeness of Hawthorne, as well as of what it calls the School of the West and South—Bret Harte, George Cable, and Mary Murfree. Lifelike portraiture is not enough, since art demands poetry, impressionism, sentiment, and 'breadth of sympathy'.[2]

A final type of criticism of James and Howells—that their realism neglects artistic conventions and selectivity—is less common than any of the foregoing, most of which pay some respect, even in passing, to their constructive merits. The *Spectator*, on the other hand, detects in James's *Confidence* the inartistic confusions of real life: 'He does not much trouble himself to contrive intricate plots, or to imagine strange situations; but he cuts a slice out of life almost at haphazard, and then goes about to reveal and analyse its constituent parts'—a method which suffers from the ultimate disadvantage that 'few human lives are so completely rounded as to give opportunity for an artistic *dénouement*'.[3] And the same periodical reviews *Washington Square* in terms which reveal the heightening and shaping effects expected of the novel: '. . . it interests him much more to paint the various aimless ways in which human beings get almost involuntarily into a sort of entanglement with each other, than to paint the course of a series of events which show the natural development of strong character, and the natural resultant of the encounter between conflicting purposes and complicated circumstances.'[4]

[1] 1896 (ii), 597.
[2] 'American Fiction', clxxiii (1891), 31–65 (by R. E. Prothero).
[3] liii (1880), 48–49. [4] liv (1881), 185–6 (by R. H. Hutton).

Finally, in an interesting review by William Sharp of Howells's *A Hazard of New Fortunes* in 1890, this selection arising out of the internal laws of the novel is linked with the essential workings of the imagination. Like Tolstoi, Howells suffers from a 'radical inability to focus essential and unessential details into one quintessential picture', and his 'pseudo-realism' is compared with the true realism that is based on artistic and illusive compression:

Perhaps realism in literary art may be approximately defined as the science of exact presentment of many complexities, abstract and concrete, in one truthful, because absolutely reasonable and apparently inevitable, synthesis; this, *plus* the creative energy which in high development involves what is misleadingly called the romantic spirit, and *minus* that weakness of the selective faculty which is the dominant factor in the work of the so-called realists of the Zolaesque school. Thus regarded, realism and romance are found to be as indissoluble as soul and body in a living human being. The true artist, no doubt, is he who is neither a realist nor a romanticist, but in whose work is observable the shaping power of the higher qualities of the methods of genuine realism and the higher qualities of the methods of genuine romance.[1]

Compared with James and Howells, it is striking how criticism of Zola is dominated by the moral issue. Nearly all are agreed on the squalor of his material, but only a few are able to condemn it as unpleasing, or untrue, or inartistic for reasons other than those of social morality. Some, like Andrew Lang in the *Fortnightly*, are content to wrinkle their nose, deny the validity of the hideous in art, complain that *Le Ventre de Paris* 'smells of pork and onions', and sigh for the days of good old Sir Walter.[2] Saintsbury goes out of his way to condemn the school on non-ethical grounds, pointing to his admiration for Baudelaire and for Maupassant's *Boule de Suif* as proof that he is not squeamish, and maintains that his objection is simply to their unpleasantness and lack of amusement. Zola, for all his

[1] *Academy*, xxxvii (1890), 41–42.
[2] 'Émile Zola', xxxi, n.s. (1882), 439–52.

merits, breaks the first rule of art, which is to present reality not as it is, but transformed and '*dis*realised'; and when his method descends to his followers, who lack his rude vigour, its weakness is revealed in their resultant dullness and futility.[1]

But most hostile criticisms arise out of a difference in moral or philosophical view-point, and the lack of idealism or of 'true realism' for which Zola is alternately blamed has little relevance to any non-moral theory of representation in the novel. It follows that the frequent assertions that he is false to real life can hardly be considered part of any trend in favour of mimetic accuracy so much as a simple denial of his ideas about human nature. For example, Arthur Symons's scornful attack in 1893 could at first sight be a realist's dismissal of all that is imaginative, subjective, and conventional in literature:

The art of Zola is nature seen through a formula. . . . He observes, indeed, with astonishing minuteness, but he observes in support of preconceived ideas. And so powerful is his imagination that he has created a whole world which has no existence anywhere but in his own brain, and he has placed there imaginary beings, so much more logical than life, in the midst of surroundings which are themselves so real as to lend almost a semblance of reality to the embodied formulas who inhabit them.[2]

Yet the article is obviously not aimed against idealism in general, but against the 'distorted' kind into which Zola has been led by his beliefs being different from those of Symons.

More relevantly, the naturalist doctrine of impersonality was attacked on the grounds of the essentially subjective nature of the artistic process. For example, Karl Hillebrand's reasons for disliking the school are widely shared: that is, its claim to create art by the methods of science, and its failure to realize that art is based instead on personal intuition, the impressionism by which alone artistic truth is achieved.[3] In 1889 the *Westminster*

[1] 'The Present State of the Novel. II', *Fortnightly Rev.* xliii, n.s. (1888), 112–23.

[2] 'A Note on Zola's Method' (1893), *Studies in Two Literatures*, 1897, pp. 204–17.

[3] 'About Old and New Novels', *Contemporary Rev.* xlv (1884), 391-5.

also expresses approval for the intrusion of the creator's temperament, but points out that Zola himself was unable to fulfil the objectivity of his formula: '. . . the temperament of the writer always intervenes to prevent him from copying nature faithfully and dispassionately.'[1]

This supposed betrayal by Zola of his own theories is seized on by many critics, and produces some of the most interesting items in the whole field of Zola criticism. The approach to Zola as an idealist *malgré lui* frees such critics from the onus of condemning him morally, and allows them to examine the techniques by which his paradoxical idealism is achieved.

Some of the accounts indicate little more than the characteristic desire for what is more intense, more imaginative, more 'poetic' than real life, as when Garnet Smith, no friend of the naturalists, sees Zola as essentially a romantic, with 'epical qualities' that conflict strangely with this theories,[2] and when the *Scots Observer* and Vernon Lee both identify him with Hugo in his 'passionate lyrism'.[3] However, two other issues emerge which receive fuller exposition: firstly, Zola's idealism in his pursuit of the universal and the abstract; and secondly, his formal—and non-naturalistic—processes of selection and arrangement.

George Moore is one who identifies Zola's idealizing talent by his use of general truths and social ideas; and in 1892 he regrets that *La Débacle* shows signs of this talent being submerged in excessive pictorial description: '. . . for his imagination is of such quality that it gains strength by strict observance of the general laws which govern humanity.'[4] In the following year

[1] 'Naturalism', cxxxii (1889), 186. Zola always protested that such 'arguments imbéciles' ignored the recognition in naturalist theory of the modifying medium of the artist's temperament (*Le Roman expérimental*, Paris, 1893, p. 10); but it is hardly surprising that his over-statement of the scientific analogy engrossed his critics' attention.

[2] 'Gustave Flaubert', *Gentleman's Mag.* cclxv (1888), 127. Even Maupassant, in 1883, had described Zola's inescapable romanticism of temperament and of method (*Émile Zola*, Paris, 1883, pp. 15–20).

[3] 'Modern Men. Émile Zola', iii (1889–90), 262–3; 'On Literary Composition', *Contemporary Rev.* lxviii (1895), 418.

[4] 'La Débacle', *Fortnightly Rev.* lii, n.s. (1892), 204–10.

G. W. Steevens, in a very valuable article, elaborates on this aspect of Zola the non-realist. All art must be governed by an idea: perhaps an aspect of human psychology, as in Balzac and Flaubert, or, as in Zola, something more abstract and philosophical. He deals not with man, but with 'man in relation to the forces that fashion the world'; and out of this approach comes a specific technique. With all the 'passion of a poet', he shows abstract and universal truths struggling to manifest themselves through his individual characters, machines, and institutions; and it is the very grandeur of these ideas that often saves their representation from being merely melodramatic: 'It is this symmetry and coherence—the constant sense of massive agencies working through all casual actions to which they lend purport and explanation—that gives us leave to call Zola the most ideal of the idealists. The real subject of the *Rougon-Macquart* is eternal truth, its real hero indestructible force.'[1]

Among those who pick out the idealizing process of selection and formal arrangement in Zola's method, George Moore is again noteworthy. In his 1885 Preface to *Piping Hot!*, the translation of *Pot-Bouille*, he mentions an obviously improbable situation in the book:

> Émile Zola has then done no more than to exaggerate, to draw the strings that attach the different parts a little tighter than they would be in nature. Art, let there be no mistake on this point, be it romantic or naturalistic, is a perpetual concession; and the character of the artist is determined by the selection he makes amid the mass of conflicting issues that, all clamouring equally to be chosen, present themselves to his mind.[2]

And elsewhere, he deprecates the critical emphasis on the Frenchman's realism: '. . . Zola's novels are poems, and have nothing to do with realism. If you seek a synthesis, you pass from observation into poetry and philosophy; and Zola's work is as obviously and as wholly synthetical as Victor Hugo's.' His strength lies not in description, the rendering of surface, but in

[1] 'Zola', *National Observer*, x (1893), 329–31. [2] p. xiv.

creating the illusion of life through his formal power of lifting detail into intense relief.[1]

Finally, two valuable analyses of Zola's technique, by J. A. Symonds in 1891 and by Havelock Ellis in 1896, are evidence not only of his admission to the fold during the nineties, but also of the increasing attention being paid to such matters at that period.[2] For Symonds, *La Bête Humaine* is 'the poem of the railway', as a railway-engine provides 'the unity of subject, movement, composition, interest, which constitutes a creation of idealizing art, and distinguishes that from the haphazard incompleteness of reality'. Every incident is chosen to sustain the central idea, and complete accuracy of motive and of surrounding detail blinds us to the unlikely conjunction of events and compression of time. It is the 'constructive imagination' which has so perfectly manipulated life into art: 'If that be not the essence of idealism—this working of the artist's brain not in but on the subject-matter of the external world and human nature—I do not know what meaning to give to the term.'[3]

The conventional nature of the novels is also brought out by Ellis, in order to dispose of the idea of absolute realism. All art is selection, and on this basis Zola is as much an idealist as George Sand. The relevant questions are rather: 'Has the artist selected his materials rightly? Has he selected them with due restraint?' Often with Zola the answer is no: 'He has left far too much of the scaffolding standing amid his huge literary structures; there is too much mere brute fact which has not been wrought into art.' But his skill can triumph over this ponderous method: '. . . in his most characteristic novels, as "L'Assom-

[1] 'Le Rêve', *Impressions and Opinions*, 1891, pp. 122–9. For Moore on Zola's method, see also below, p. 120.

[2] They also indicate that Moore's attention to the formal organization of Zola's novels would not have seemed totally 'eccentric' in his time, as Graham Hough suggests ('George Moore and the Nineties', *Edwardians and Late Victorians*, ed. R. Ellmann, New York, 1960, p. 22).

[3] '*La Bête Humaine*. A Study in Zola's Idealism', *Fortnightly Rev.* l, n.s. (1891), 453–62. For Symonds's views on the essential ideality of all art, see 'Realism and Idealism', in *Essays, Speculative and Suggestive*, 1890, i, 168–98.

moir'', ''Nana'', ''Germinal'', his efforts to attain salient perspective in the mass of trivial or technical details—to build a single elaborate effect out of manifold details—are often admirably conducted.' Frequently, he uses the repetition of a formula, like the monstrous figure of Voreux, the coal-pit in *Germinal*:

> It is more than the tricky repetition of a word or a gesture, overdone by Dickens and others; it is the artful manipulation of a carefully-elaborated, significant phrase. Zola seems to have been the first who has, deliberately and systematically, introduced this sort of *leit-motiv* into literature as a method of summarising a complex mass of details, and bringing the impression of them before the reader. In this way he contrives to minimise the defects of his method, and to render his complex detail focal.[1]

It shows once again the strength of the idealist tradition among English novel-critics that where Zola is not openly attacked for his scientific and inartistic realism, he is so often transformed into a visionary or a selective artist.

VII. THE RISE OF THE ROMANCE

The distinction between the romance and the novel is as old as the beginnings of prose fiction. Clara Reeve's *The Progress of Romance* in 1785 is one *locus classicus*: 'The Romance is an heroic fable, which treats of fabulous persons and things.—The Novel is a picture of real life and manners, and of the times in which it is written. The Romance in lofty and elevated language, describes what never happened nor is likely to happen.—The Novel gives a familiar relation of such things, as pass every day before our eyes, such as may happen to our friend, or to ourselves'[2]—a basic account which reappears at times throughout the nineteenth century, and is even accepted by many modern critics.[3] To believe that romance is one possible element of

[1] 'Zola: the Man and his Work', *Savoy*, i (1896), 67–71.

[2] i, 111.

[3] e.g. René Wellek and Austin Warren, *Theory of Literature*, New York, 1949, pp. 223–4; Richard Chase, *The American Novel and its Tradition*, New York, 1957, pp. 12–13; and Northrop Frye, *Anatomy of Criticism*, Princeton, 1957, pp. 303–14.

fiction, or a separate form of it, is not necessarily to challenge the mimetic approach. But the possibilities of conflict are obviously there, and when in the later part of the century anti-realist critics found the romance being fully revived in its own right, they made its name into a battle-cry.

In the sixties and seventies the word 'romance' excites little debate, but retains its own significance and potential importance. Despite the fact that J. C. Jeaffreson had written in 1858: 'The distinction that once existed between *novels* and *romances* has for a long time been lost sight of. In general conversation the two words are now used as synonymous',[1] there is plenty of evidence to the contrary in the years that follow. For example, in 1870 Disraeli's *Lothair* is praised by *Tinsley's Magazine*, despite the unreal, fanciful world it describes, on the grounds that it is not an ordinary novel, 'dealing with ordinary people in an ordinary world', but a romance, 'couleur de rose'[2]; and Mortimer Collins's *The Vivian Romance* is welcomed by the *British Quarterly* for having all the elements of unreal brilliance that its title would suggest.[3] In 1872 the fanciful extravagance of Meredith's *Harry Richmond* makes it, for one reviewer, 'not a novel, but a romance'[4]; and W. G. Palgrave's *Hermann Agha* is seen by another critic as that rare type, a complete romance, totally removed from the novel of reflection or social observation.[5] Lastly, in 1876 an article on Ouida sees this division as part of the nature of fiction:

Novels may, broadly speaking, be classed as realistic and romantic. Both take nature as their starting-point, the only difference being, that the novelist proper studies to represent his little world as the great world is; whereas the romance-writer takes some striking char-

[1] *Novels and Novelists from Elizabeth to Victoria*, 1858, i, 1. Caroline Washburn, in her unpublished survey of the earlier period, also finds no clear difference in the use of the two words by 1860 (*The History, from 1832 to 1860, of British Criticism of Prose Fiction* (Thesis Abstract), Urbana, 1937, p. 9).

[2] 'Lothair', vi (1870), 565–8.

[3] lii (1870), 538.

[4] *Westminster Rev.* xli, n.s. (1872), 274–5.

[5] *Spectator*, xlv (1872), 920–1.

acteristic in human nature, and builds an ideal world therefrom by the very force of his imagination, and that fact alone constitutes him the greater writer. A novel, therefore, in which imagination predominates, and realism is not wanting, would, by this combination, merit the highest rank.[1]

The continuous taste for romance, implicit in the many favourable accounts of these and similar writers, becomes particularly clear in reactions to Hawthorne. The American, whose novels can obviously be appreciated by no ordinary canon of realism, remains a firm favourite throughout the whole period, though at times he causes his critics some puzzlement. For example, 'Matthew Browne' (W. B. Rands) in 1871 confesses to his unease at Hawthorne's indeterminateness, the haze of mystery over all his romances—'the endless filaments of suggestion sent out in search of symbolic meanings'—but in the end accepts this as the mark of his genius. Browne admires the way in which the characters are kept human in such weird and imaginative surroundings, and how the preternatural is always kept within a natural context.[2] It is this use of romance in such a way as to reconcile realism and idealism, to attain the long-sought compromise, that seems to win such universal praise for Hawthorne. His achievement is repeatedly hailed as the successful creation of 'a site which shall be solid and life-like, and yet sufficiently far removed from the day's actualities for one to throw some light of ideality upon the creations who walk thereon'.[3] And when R. F. Littledale criticizes Julian Hawthorne's *The Laughing Mill, and Other Stories* in 1879, it is because the author has neglected his father's practice of building for his romantic edifice a plausible framework of realistic detail.[4]

Understandably, Hawthorne maintains his popularity in later years, when his romance seems all the more attractive against a background of Zolaism—or Jamesism. W. L. Courtney,

[1] 'Ouida's Novels', *Westminster Rev.* xlix, n.s. (1876), 361.

[2] 'Nathaniel Hawthorne', *Saint Paul's*, viii (1871), 157–8.

[3] Keningale Cook, 'American Novelists. III. Nathaniel Hawthorne', *Belgravia*, xix (1873), 72–79.

[4] *Academy*, xv (1879), 320.

for example, in 1886, is grateful that 'his romantic idealism . . . helps us to banish the vulgar forms of realism, as possible modes of art'.[1] And in the *Edinburgh Review*'s attack on the 'New England School' in 1891, Hawthorne is made to represent the romantic path of 'Fancy, imagination, poetic vision' from which his merely novelistic successors have strayed.[2] Lastly, Thomas Bradfield's 'The Romances of Nathaniel Hawthorne' in the *Westminster* for 1894, with its enthusiasm for his qualities of mystery and unreality, his drawing of souls rather than bodies, and his arrival through the intuitive imagination at ultimate truth and lofty beauty, is a fitting climax of praise for a writer whose self-confessed romances seemed to so many critics over the years the embodiment of the highest qualities of idealism.[3]

The challenge of the new realists in the early eighties brings the romance quite dramatically into the foreground of controversy, almost as a rediscovered genre. To Saintsbury, one of its great partisans, the word implies 'a story dealing more with adventure and with the tragic passions than with analytic character-drawing and observation of manners'[4]; and for great numbers of critics in the same year, 1881, these criteria were strikingly fulfilled in the appearance of J. H. Shorthouse's *John Inglesant*. The *Saturday* took the author's use of 'Romance' in his sub-title as a link with Hawthorne, suggesting as it did 'a greater latitude of poetic and imaginative treatment', an appeal to the few rather than the many, and to a 'more subtle and unusual range of feelings', compared with 'the novel proper'.[5]

In the following year the name of Stevenson appears in the same magazine as the hoped-for leader of a romantic renaissance that will lift contemporary fiction above the level of mere 'annals of the boudoir and the tennis-lawn'.[6] Stevenson needed no urging—nor did he need the *Saturday* to defend his cause,

[1] 'Hawthorne's Romances', *Fortnightly Rev.* xl, n.s. (1886), 516.
[2] 'American Fiction', clxxiii (1891), 47–51 (by R. E. Prothero).
[3] cxlii (1894), 203–14.
[4] *Academy*, xix (1881), 204.
[5] lii (1881), 50–51.
[6] 'The Modern Novel', liv (1882), 633–4.

being quite the most articulate of the new romancists. His 'A Humble Remonstrance' (1884) is a public statement of the aims of the school, in formal disagreement with the realism represented by Henry James. Contrary to what James has said (in 'The Art of Fiction') the novel cannot compete with life, Stevenson insists, but turns away from it: 'Our art is occupied, and bound to be occupied, not so much in making stories true as in making them typical.' The young writer, 'in this age of the particular', should aim to produce not a copy but 'a simplification of some side or point of life'.[1] Realism is nothing more than a subsidiary technique, which, he declares elsewhere, even the romancer can utilize on occasion; and it is the modern school's failure to realize this that has caused its downfall: 'Beware of realism; it is the devil; 'tis one of the means of art, and now they make it the end!'[2] In 1893 he bewails in a letter to Henry James the realistic tendencies of the genre: 'How to get over, how to escape from, the besotting *particularity* of fiction. "Roland approached the house; it had green doors and window blinds; and there was a scraper on the upper step." To hell with Roland and the scraper!'[3] Romance tries to escape this, offering 'the poetry of circumstance', and thereby, Stevenson goes on, 'the great creative writer shows us the realisation and the apotheosis of the daydreams of common men. His stories may be nourished with the realities of life, but their true mark is to satisfy the nameless longings of the reader and to obey the ideal laws of the daydream.'[4]

Stevenson has much to say on the artist's need for realism of this ancillary kind. He praises James's *The Princess Casamassima* for being more realistic than his other works, for its 'grime' and 'emphasis of skeleton'.[5] And with his ineradicable Scots pragmatism he frequently shows a concern for authenticity in his own writing: '. . . with all my romance, I am a realist and a

[1] *Longman's Mag.* v (1884–5), 139–47.
[2] *Letters*, ed. S. Colvin, 1911, ii, 125. [3] ibid. iv, 199.
[4] 'A Gossip on Romance', *Longman's Mag.* i (1882–3), 69–79.
[5] *Letters*, ii, 251.

prosaist, and a most fanatical lover of plain physical sensations plainly and expressly rendered; hence my perils'.[1] But his distrust of the perils is predominant, and the doctrine he continues to preach is one of romantic modification.

The daydream is not the only principle of romance, however. There is also Stevenson's famous obsession with the technique of writing, his perpetual demand for the processes of omission and organization which in themselves set the novel far apart from life:

> Life is monstrous, infinite, illogical, abrupt, and poignant; a work of art, in comparison, is neat, finite, self-contained, rational, flowing, and emasculate. . . . The novel which is a work of art exists, not by its resemblances to life, which are forced and material, as a shoe must still consist of leather, but by its immeasurable difference from life, which is designed and significant, and is both the method and the meaning of the work.[2]

A further means of idealization always stressed by Stevenson is the spirit, the philosophic tenor, of the work, and in this he speaks for many of his fellow-theorists of the nineteenth-century romance: 'As I live, I feel more and more that literature should be cheerful and brave-spirited, even if it cannot be made beautiful and pious and heroic. We wish it to be a green place.'[3] The Stevensonian romance must be a thing of shape and artifice, but it needs the further modifying qualities of vitality, charm, and magnanimity to do battle with the realist 'Daemon of the epoch'.[4]

In many ways 1887 is the year of recognition for the new romance: Saintsbury, Rider Haggard, and Andrew Lang all issue manifestos on its behalf. The former welcomes the decline of

[1] *Letters*, iv, 49. He was acutely aware of these apparent dangers: the outcry of reviewers that in *The Ebb-Tide* he had turned to the false gods of realism was anticipated by Stevenson himself, who agonizes in his letters over the sordidness and the un-romantic treatment which that book had forced on him.

[2] 'A Humble Remonstrance', *Longman's Mag*. v (1884–5), 142–3. See also 'A Note on Realism', *Magazine of Art*, vii (1883–4), 24–28.

[3] *Letters*, ii, 172–3. [4] ibid. iii, 42.

monotonous 'manners-painting and refined character-analysis' before the onset of Stevenson and Haggard, with their concentration on the poetic features of character and incident. In Saintsbury's eyes, the romance, which flourishes best in a period of change, is the key to all social and literary dynamism. Only through it can the *essence* of man be explored, and beside it the novel is transitory and parasitic. As a result, great things will never be accomplished 'till we have bathed once more long and well in the romance of adventure and of passion'.[1]

Haggard (despite some disingenuous modesty) is hardly less sweeping in his claims: '. . . with the exception of perfect sculpture, really good romance writing is perhaps the most difficult art practised by the sons of men.' People are longing to escape from the horrors of French naturalism and the 'laboured nothingness' of the emasculate American school. The romance, despite its detractors, can provide the answer: it will transport readers into the realms of beauty and heroism, away from mere cerebration and problems of good and evil. The romance's world of pure imagination is timeless, and men will read the *Arabian Nights* and *Robinson Crusoe* long after realism—and Mr. Howells—have passed from memory.[2] And in the same year Andrew Lang, after disparaging the vulgarity of the whole controversy, produces his own characteristic declaration: 'The dubitations of a Bostonian spinster may be made as interesting, by one genius, as a fight between a crocodile and a catawampus, by another genius. . . . But if there is to be no *modus vivendi*, if the battle between the crocodile of Realism and the catawampus of Romance is to be fought out to the bitter end—why, in that Ragnarôk, I am on the side of the Catawampus.'[3]

When the *Westminster* hails Rider Haggard's article as evidence of a 'romantic revival', it goes on to suggest a new name as one of the standard-bearers, that of Hall Caine:

[1] 'The Present State of the Novel. I', *Fortnightly Rev.* xlii, n.s. (1887), 410–17.

[2] 'About Fiction', *Contemporary Rev.* li (1887), 172–80.

[3] 'Realism and Romance', ibid. lii (1887), 683-93.

This power of transmuting the ordinary into the marvellous by means of an imaginative manipulation which, though daring and vivid, yet keeps itself within the bounds of the truly artistic, is the main factor of differentiation between the novel and the romance. The distinction has grown to be less insisted upon than in the days of Nathaniel Hawthorne, but it is by no means a distinction without a difference; and Mr. Hall Caine has traversed the boundary with eminent skill.[1]

Once brought forward, Caine is happy to wave the flag; and by 1890 he has produced a highly-coloured essay, 'The New Watchwords of Fiction', which might be taken as representing the extreme of the idealist position, and the high-water mark of romance theory. The moral basis of the romance is important to Caine, and Justice and Faith are prominent among the watchwords; but he is also concerned with the ideals of Imagination, Beauty, and Passion. He pours scorn on the belief that realism is the more fitting tendency in the modern age, and on Zola's lack of the imagination and enthusiasm vital to idealism: 'I take realism to mean the doctrine of the importance of the real facts of life, and idealism the doctrine of the superiority of ideal existence over the facts of life.' To omit from the novel all that is uncommon, startling, colourful, as Zola would appear to wish, is to confuse the novelist wth the historian. For the novelist, fact is only an aid towards the display of passion, and his true concern must be with the mysteries of human nature in its highest development—that is, in the regions of heroism. Caine proceeds to his peroration after quoting Bacon, Burton, and Goethe in his support: 'And I would add for myself as the essence of my creed as a novelist: *Fiction is not nature, it is not character, it is not imagined history; it is fallacy, poetic fallacy, pathetic fallacy, a lie if you like, a beautiful lie, a lie that is at once false and true—false to fact, true to faith.*'

After a further description of the moral grandeur of romance, he ends in a trumpet-blast against realism, which has had its day and is disgraced. France has abandoned its vile Zola, and looks for some new Messiah of idealism; Russia has found hers in

[1] 'A New Novelist', cxxviii (1887), 840–9.

Tolstoi; even in America, Howells is turning romantic. The whole world is waiting, and the millenium of romanticism is at hand.[1]

Hall Caine's optimism was hardly to be borne out, for the romance's stream of talent was a thin one. Haggard, for example, attracted as much hostility as admiration, and was bludgeoned in many such articles as William Watson's 'The Fall of Fiction'.[2] And there were some like D. F. Hannigan, in the *Westminster* for 1894, who dismissed all romance as a decadent form in an age of splendid realism: 'We are sick of lying and cant and platitude. We want facts, not romantic dreams.'[3] Yet the majority of critics through the nineties, while admitting that the serious novel of realistic psychology or portraiture of manners was more in keeping with the spirit of the times, and more likely to succeed, believed that the romance had its peculiar and valid aims that deserved better exponents.[4] Frederic Harrison, looking back with nostalgia at the literature of a previous generation, accepted that the modern realist tendency would produce true art, of a limited sort, but regretted that Socialism and a unified culture were against the passion, incident, variety, colour, and individuality that are the essence of romance.[5] And others, like G. S. Street in 1898, expressed the wish that Stevenson, out of all the rest, had lived to demonstrate the full possibility of the form—'For our sham revivals of cloak and dagger are poor things.'[6]

By the admission of many of these critics, the revival of the romance was largely based on the yearning for escape. As such, it was clearly moving against the current not just of contemporary realism, but of the whole development of fiction over the

[1] *Contemporary Rev.* lvii (1890), 479–88.

[2] *Fortnightly Rev.* xliv, n.s. (1888), 324-36 (identified by Professor James G. Nelson of the University of Wisconsin).

[3] 'The Decline of Romance', cxli (1894), 33–36.

[4] e.g. 'Novels of Adventure and Manners', *Quarterly Rev.* clxxix (1894), 530–52; and 'Romanticism and Realism', *Saturday Rev.* lxxviii (1894), 615–16.

[5] *Studies in Early Victorian Literature*, 1895, pp. 22–39.

[6] 'Some Opinions', *Blackwood's Edinburgh Mag.* clxiv (1898), 600.

succeeding generations. Nevertheless, it has a significance beyond that of the *Boy's Own* yarns it actually produced, in that it served to dramatize the antinomy in English novel-theory. Anthony Hope's exposition in 1897 of the aims of his school gave good expression to certain perennial (and not invalid) desires of English readers, and to one of the two poles, idealism and realism, between which the age's criticism flowed:

> [The romance] can give to love an ideal object, to ambition a boundless field, to courage a high occasion; and these great emotions, revelling in their freedom, exhibit themselves in their glory. Thus in its most worthy forms, in the hands of its masters, it can not only delight men, but can touch them to the very heart. It shows them what they would be if they could, if time and fate and circumstances did not bind, what in a sense they all are, and what their acts would show them to be if an opportunity offered. So they dream and are the happier, and at least none the worse for their dreams.[1]

[1] Quoted in Sir Charles Mallet, *Anthony Hope and his Books*, 1935, p. 114.

3

MORALS, IDEAS, AND THE NOVEL

PROBABLY the best-known preoccupation of Victorian aesthetics is with the moral nature of art. Its general effect on literary taste and reputations, the battles of Mrs. Grundy, the trial of Henry Vizetelly, the rebels of the *Yellow Book*, all have been adequately and interestingly described elsewhere.[1] But the more precise question remains of how, in the eyes of critics, moral utility affected the novel's very nature. How, they ask, can a novel properly express a code of values, so as to steer between the extremes of open didacticism and complete amorality? Their obsessive concern for the relationship of art and morality is easily guyed, but cannot be dismissed as irrelevant. For all the limitations of their enquiry, they were confronting a problem which is still largely unanswered and which is still vital to an understanding of art: the exact nature of a literary 'idea'.

I. THE NOVELIST IN THE PULPIT

In the period after 1865, the insistence on moral teaching is at its crudest and most vigorous over the first fifteen years, and the reviewers' endless chorus of 'bracing', 'healthy', and 'wholesome' makes the novel sound like a seaside-resort for the soul. *Tinsley's Magazine* in 1873 defines the true function of the novel as the illustration of moral principles 'in their practical working', and the teaching of lessons in religion, politics, and social philosophy, 'not merely in dry dissertation, but in vivid and humanised description'. The writer welcomes the conscious

[1] e.g. C. R. Decker, *The Victorian Conscience*, New York, 1952; W. C. Frierson, 'The English Controversy Over Realism in Fiction, 1885–1895', *P.M.L.A.* xliii (1928), 533–50; and Malcolm Elwin, *Old Gods Falling*, 1939.

purpose he detects in Lytton's *Kenelm Chillingly* and George Eliot's *Middlemarch*, and defines the latter, with approval, as 'a homily against ill-assorted marriages'.[1] In the same strain, the *Saturday* sets the novel the task of 'elevating the character by setting before the reader great aims and ennobling conceptions of life'[2]; and the *British Quarterly Review* often defends direct purpose and religious didacticism from the 'higher criticism' that attacks it,[3] and frequently champions George MacDonald for ignoring such minor matters as 'success or failure in the construction of his plots' in favour of presenting the moral ideal.[4]

In Trollope, the view reaches its apotheosis: 'I have ever thought of myself as a preacher of sermons, and my pulpit as one which I could make both salutary and agreeable to my audience.'[5] The novelist, he admits, must certainly aim at being convincing and pleasing, but ultimately and unavoidably, 'The object of a novel should be to instruct in morals while it amuses'.[6] Once the knack of sugaring the pill is mastered, according to Trollope, little more remains to be said about morality in fiction, and he is free to load his criticism with such praise as, of Jane Austen, 'a sweet lesson of homely household womanly virtue is ever being taught',[7] and with his perpetual invocations to the cheek of the maiden person.

After Trollope's death in 1882, the search for a simple and direct moral message is found mainly in articles of an obviously conservative, pietistic bent—though the number of these is worth noting. The welcome given by the *Westminster* to Hall Caine in 1887 is partly because he has managed to 'exemplify in romance the higher and nobler teachings of moral duty'.[8]

[1] 'The Theory of Fiction', xiii (1873), 88–92.

[2] 'The Uses of Fiction', xxii (1866), 323–4.

[3] e.g. lx (1874), 266–7.

[4] e.g. 'Works by George MacDonald', xlvii (1868), 21; and lv (1872), 265–6.

[5] *An Autobiography*, 1883, i, 195 (Chapter 8).

[6] *Thackeray*, 1879, p. 109.

[7] 'On English Prose Fiction as a Rational Amusement' (1870), *Four Lectures*, ed. M. L. Parrish, 1938, p. 105.

[8] 'A New Novelist', cxxviii (1887), 848.

And in 1893 Francis Marion Crawford insists that the novelist should go beyond realism 'by showing men what they may be, ought to be, or can be', and that 'The foundation of good fiction and good poetry seems to be ethic rather than aesthetic'.[1] The *Dublin Review* in 1886 offers a final example of this moral attitude at its most extreme, in C. C. Longridge's remarkable 'Novelists and Novels', an article which could have been written a century before:

The object, therefore, which the writer of fiction should always hold in view is to exercise the phantasy in pleasant but lawful subjects, to fill it with novel and happy images, and by this indirect, as well as by a direct, appeal to the heart, so to temper and control the passions as may be most suitable to the formation of virtue and the extirpation of vice. For this reason, his representations should be chaste, his sentiments pure, and his leading characters noble-minded and virtuous.[2]

The concept that fiction is a means of edification, however, is taken over by the 'new didacticism' of the eighties and nineties, and used with reference to the dissemination of ideas of every kind rather than the upholding of a traditional ethic. The instance alone of Gissing shows how the artistic conscience of the later years—at its most sensitive in him—always had to exist alongside an older belief in the artist's social responsibilities. Gissing always denied advocating any theory in his novels, yet basically he aspired, like his own artist-heroes, to be an agent of social and moral reform. He wrote to his brother in 1880: 'I mean to bring home to people the ghastly condition (material, mental, and moral) of our poor classes, to show the hideous injustice of our whole system of society, to give light upon the plan of altering it, and, above all, to preach an enthusiasm for just and high *ideals* in this age of unmitigated egotism and "shop". I shall never write a book which does not keep all these ends in view.'[3]

[1] *The Novel, What It Is*, pp. 77, 86.

[2] xvi (1886), 1–9.

[3] *Letters of George Gissing to Members of his Family*, ed. A. and E. Gissing, 1927, p. 83. For more on Gissing's divided allegiance, see below, pp. 87-88; and Jacob Korg, 'Division of Purpose in George Gissing', *P.M.L.A.* lxx (1955), 323–36.

Throughout the period, then, there is a widespread sense that the novel has an outright moral or philosophical function—but critics differ in how they interpret it. Most commonly, they do so in the familiar Victorian terms of a vague ethical idealism, as when Arabella Shore praises Meredith for penetrating to the 'truth of things', and aiding in 'the great task of social regeneration' by uncovering the 'noble ideal' and 'the eternal moral code' that lie beneath the mere phenomena of life.[1] Meredith's own conception of the place of values in the novel is similarly idealist. As an enemy of the conventional prudery implied in the word 'morality', he uses instead such words as 'philosophy', 'thought', 'problems of life', 'the Spirit', and 'Idea' to describe his aims. The novel, he holds, must be an instrument of Civilization and the Comic Spirit, opposed to scientific materialism, and uncovering 'the laws of existence' and 'the destinies of the world'.[2]

George Moore, like Meredith, is thought of most commonly as a crusader against prudery and moral censorship[3]; but he, too, seems to allow for certain high moral absolutes being part of the nature of art. His demands in the novel are for 'seriousness', 'depth of life', and 'thought', by which he means not only a freer choice of subject-matter and a profounder psychology, but also the saying of 'profound things on profound subjects', and the use, as in Tolstoi, of characters for their moral as well as their social significance.[4] In spite of typically inconsistent attacks on moral purpose,[5] he continues to apply some moral standard of his own in criticizing Flaubert's 'odious pessimism',[6] and in disapproving of Kipling because 'the anecdote that does not represent a moral idea, however curious, however exciting,

[1] 'The Novels of George Meredith', *British Quarterly Rev.* lxix (1879), 411–25.

[2] e.g. *Letters*, ed. W. M. Meredith, 1912, ii, 398; Lionel Stevenson, *The Ordeal of George Meredith*, New York, 1953, p. 193; and *Diana of the Crossways*, Memorial Edn., 1910, pp. 15–20 (Chapter 1).

[3] e.g. in *Literature at Nurse*, 1885; and 'A New Censorship of Literature', *Pall Mall Gazette*, xl (10 December 1884), 1–2.

[4] 'Since the Elizabethans', *Cosmopolis*, iv (1896), 42–58.

[5] e.g. on Tolstoi, in *Avowals*, 1919, pp. 152–64.

[6] *Confessions of a Young Man*, 1888, p. 297.

can never rise to the height of great literature'.[1] The nature of this overriding moral order is not gone into, nor is the technique of its application. Moore's energies (perhaps just as profitably at the time) are spent on arguing that this morality of art, whatever its details, is certainly not the morality of British Matrondom: 'That there are great and eternal moral laws which must be acted up to in art as in life I am more than ready to admit; but these are very different from the wretched conventionalities which have been arbitrarily imposed upon us in England.'[2]

Lastly, W. S. Lilly provides a very typical specimen of how the moral idealist reacted to French naturalism in the eighties, in his assertion that the duty of art is to contradict science by presenting 'that image of a fairer and better world, the desire of which springs eternal in the human breast'. The novelist must present the Good, observe the 'great ethical principles of reserve, shame, reverence', and concentrate on the soul : '. . . the true value of any work of art is its ethical value, and . . . the measure of its ethical value is its correspondence with the truth of things. But the true is the ideal; the phenomenal is not the real, but its perpetual antithesis.'[3]

Some other accounts of the morality of fiction are more empirical, centred on the notion of an unchanging community of shared belief—the sanction here being society rather than the 'truth of things'. J. M. Robertson, for example, criticizing W. D. Howells's view of life in 1884, describes the rapport essential to the novelist: '. . . his effects depend on a general harmony between his views of life and those of his readers. A certain moral code is understood between them and him, and this code is really part of his material. This being so, it is scarcely possible that he should be without ethical purpose.'[4] And similarly,

[1] Preface to Dostoevsky's *Poor Folk*, 1894, p. vii. For one account of Moore as a basically conventional moralist, see W. C. Frierson, 'George Moore Compromised with the Victorians', *Trollopian*, i (1947), 37–44.

[2] Preface to Zola's *Piping Hot!* (*Pot-Bouille*), 1885, p. xv.

[3] 'The New Naturalism', *Fortnightly Rev.* xxxviii, n.s. (1885), 240–56.

[4] 'Mr. Howells' Novels', *Westminster Rev.* lxvi, n.s. (1884), 357–75. The idea is expanded in his 'Science in Criticism', *Essays Towards a Critical Method*, 1889, pp. 2–148 (where the essay on Howells also appears).

Arthur Waugh, in the *Yellow Book*, defines the limits of the morally permissible in art as those observed by the cultured conversation of the day, steering between 'the prudery of the manse' and 'the effrontery of the pot-house'. We must judge as to the presence or absence of the essential moral idea by whether the work makes for 'that standard of taste which is normal to wholesomeness and sanity of judgment', and whether it encourages us to the line of conduct recommended 'by the experience of the age'.[1]

The demand for exclusion on the grounds of social convention is often at its most crass, surprisingly enough, in the nineties, when many critics reacted against the new enlargement of the frontiers of art. In 1890 Walter Besant, who speaks at times as the very mouthpiece of Philistine and insular England, puts the viewpoint unblushingly. He erects 'that great authority, Average Opinion' into a complete artistic guide, and sees its proscription of any portrayal of illicit love as being simply based on the facts: '. . . let us not forget that the cultured class of British women—a vast and continually increasing class—are entirely to be trusted. Rare, indeed, is it that an Englishman of this class is jealous of his wife: never does he suspect his bride.'[2] James Ashcroft Noble in 1895 calls his authority 'civilization', and compares the reticence it imposes on literature in sexual matters to the custom in 'civilized' society of putting toilets in distant parts of the house.[3] And *Temple Bar*, also in 1895, cites as evidence of the moral depravity of contemporary fiction such a breach of normal social decorum as characters discussing the legs of ballet-dancers in mixed company.[4]

It is strange that more critics, seeking a middle way for the novel between moral restrictiveness and anarchy, did not suggest some kind of wide humanistic ethic as its guiding

[1] 'Reticence in Literature', i (1894), 201–19.

[2] 'Candour in English Fiction', *New Rev.* ii (1890), 6–9.

[3] 'The Fiction of Sexuality', *Contemporary Rev.* lxvii (1895), 494–8. See also his *Morality in English Fiction* (1886), which, in its adulation of George Eliot, is one of the clearest instances of ethical idealism as a ruling principle of criticism.

[4] 'The Modern Novel', cv (1895), 248.

principle—like, for example, Eneas Sweetland Dallas's theory, in 1866, of a special 'natural' morality for poetry, based on the heart's affections rather than conscience or duty.[1] Walter Raleigh is one who does make a move towards this when he praises the 'wise and beautiful morality' of Stevenson:

> A novel cannot, of course, be moral as an action is moral; there is no question in art of police regulations or conformity to established codes, but rather of insight both deep and wide. . . . The romancer is not bound to display allegiance to particular moral laws of the kind that can be broken; he is bound to show his consciousness of that wider moral order which can no more be broken by crime than the law of gravitation can be broken by the fall of china—the morality without which life would be impossible; the relations, namely, of human beings to each other, the feelings, habits, and thoughts that are the web of society. For the appreciation of morality in this wider sense high gifts of imagination are necessary.[2]

But for most critics, this 'wider moral order' remains the prerogative of poetry. The novel is clearly felt to be bound by different rules, due, no doubt, to its supposedly influential position in society, and to its greater reliance on material drawn from the everyday world of moral situations and decisions—as well as its comparative lack of pedigree. The moral ideal, or a specifically Christian ideal, or, most frequently, a belief in the absolute nature of the social code, continues to dominate most accounts of the relationship of fiction to values right to the end of the century. The national sense of outrage at French naturalism came from this belief in the novel's attachment to certain indisputable ethical truths. The new fiction was honestly feared as the harbinger of a chaos that was more than literary: 'Lewd, and bold, and bare, living for lust and lusting for this life and its good things, and naught beyond, the heroines of realism dance, with Bacchanalian revellings, across the astonished stage of literature.'[3] And James Payn, finally, put a plain man's

[1] *The Gay Science*, 1866, ii, 192–3.

[2] *Robert Louis Stevenson*, 1895, pp. 62–64.

[3] H. Rider Haggard, 'About Fiction', *Contemporary Rev.* li (1887), 176–7.

request in 1899 which was the request all plain men made of literature, and above all of the genre which touched most closely on the aspirations, the fears, and the doubts of ordinary lives: 'What right has a man to pen a story like Turganieff's *On the Eve* to make generations of his fellow-creatures miserable? What lesson is there to be learned from it save the inscrutable cruelty of Fate? Who is the better—or even the wiser—for it?'[1] The novel's task was not only to reflect passively what was best in the values of contemporary society: it had to lead men hopefully from the pulpit towards the attainment of moral perfection. And the great cry against realist pessimism that sounds through the eighties and nineties was the complaint of a betrayed congregation.

II. THE NOVEL'S VALUES AT WORK

Critics largely ignore the question of how, in detail, the novel is to convey its message, or signify its loyalty to a code. Right and wrong, it is implied, exist as materially as a landscape, and will be represented faithfully according to the mimetic accuracy of the work. The 'balance' which is demanded, often in an analogy with painting, is less a matter of form than of 'moral realism':

> . . . *composition* is not all. We require moral perspective and moral chiaro-oscuro as well. What is trivial and incidental must not be drawn too large. What is important must not be drawn too small. And further, the lights and shades, or, if we like to add a new metaphor, the colours, must be properly harmonised and distributed. Everything must not be made an unrelieved darkness by vice or sorrow, or a flat and even brightness by joy or virtue.[2]

However, there are four ways by which critics approach a little nearer the heart of the question: by examining the supposed moral effect of the novel on the reader; the nature of the artist; his particular use of characters; and the convention of poetic justice.

[1] 'The Compleat Novelist', *The Backwater of Life*, 1899, pp. 155–6.

[2] Impressions of Theophrastus Such', *Edinburgh Rev.* cl (1879), 558 (by W. H. Mallock).

Discussions of audience-effect constantly refer to some such faculty as the 'moral sense', or to the close relation between the imaginative faculty and man's moral nature.[1] It is through their effects on these faculties that undisguised pictures of vice corrupt. For example, J. A. Noble in 1885, though recognizing the special moral teachings in Moore's *A Mummer's Wife*, points out that he achieves this by sacrificing 'something still more precious': '. . . this something assuredly *is* sacrificed when, for the sake of enforcing a mere ethical proposition, the moral nature is exposed to contamination by prolonged imaginative companionship with the very evil against which the moral warning is directed.' Moore may claim that unflinching veracity to life produces its own lessons, but propinquity with evil things deadens the moral sensibilities.[2]

Vernon Lee, as an early investigator of psychology in aesthetics, goes further. Baldwin, her spokesman in 'A Dialogue on Novels' in 1885, also disagrees with the idea that an accurate picture of life will inevitably provide moral instruction. This time the grounds are that the reader's faculties of 'the intellect, the imagination, the imaginative emotions' respond differently to art, and are dangerously sensitive to artistic representations of evil. Pictures of the physical side of love are below the range of the 'intellectual emotions', and stimulate the lower side of our nature, as in the case of Maupassant's *Une Vie*: '. . . like nine out of ten French novels, it dragged the imagination over physical details with which the imagination has no legitimate connection, which can only enervate, soil, and corrupt it.'[3]

The existence of a 'moral sense' in man is argued for by William Archer five years later, in a heated rejoinder to Oscar Wilde in the *Scots Observer*. Usually, the faculty does not interfere with our aesthetic response, Archer says, but when it does

[1] The belief is firmly in the eighteenth-century tradition, going back in part to Shaftesbury's use of the 'moral sense' as the link between intellect and sensation, and hence as the medium of didacticism in art.

[2] *Spectator*, lviii (1885), 83–85.

[3] *Contemporary Rev.* xlviii (1885), 390–401.

assert itself it is supreme: 'We cannot by an effort of the aesthetic will, so to speak, close our nostrils to moral putrescence.'[1] And Emily Crawford is typical of many—even of intelligent, unpuritanical writers like Saintsbury—in her concern for the health of this faculty when it is at its most delicate, in the young: 'How can we expect the young to escape from spring blights if that beautiful and natural guard against them, the sense which calls the mantling blush to the cheek, is broken down by literature that is wantonly prurient?'[2]

Thomas Hardy, no great believer in the young person as a yardstick, throws a different light on the moral theory of audience-effect—not from the standpoint of how corruption is to be avoided, but how the true lessons of literature are to be conveyed. The method he recommends arises out of the intuitive, anti-intellectual nature of his own beliefs. Any moral effect of fiction, he holds, should form part of the total impression of the book, and argumentative disquisitions *on* life cannot affect readers like the instinctive appeal made by pictures of life 'construed, though not distorted, by the light of imagination'. A properly dramatic presentment will avoid the pitfalls of conventional 'moral purpose' yet still 'have a sound effect' on the reader through its appeal to his whole nature, his non-logical 'intuitive conviction'.[3]

In spite of the great differences in their beliefs, there is an obvious parallel here with George Eliot, who also based her theory of the morality of fiction on the whole sensibility of the reader: 'My function is that of the *aesthetic*, not the doctrinal teacher—the rousing of the nobler emotions, which make mankind desire the social right, not the prescribing of special

[1] iv (1890), 280–1.

[2] 'Émile Zola', *Contemporary Rev.* lv (1889), 113. See Saintsbury on 'consideration for the young person' in 'The Present State of the Novel. II', *Fortnightly Rev.* xliii, n.s. (1888), 122.

[3] 'The Profitable Reading of Fiction', *Forum*, New York, v (1888), 57–70. Hardy is always indignant at those who find 'theories' in his books, claiming in the preface to *Tess* that 'the contemplative [parts are] oftener charged with impressions than with convictions' (Library Edn., 1949, p. viii).

measures, concerning which the artistic mind, however strongly moved by social sympathy, is often not the best judge.'[1]

Critics are just as concerned with the moral nature of the artist as they are with the question of audience-effect. The idea is present everywhere, often inextricably entangled with other moral issues. For George Stott, in 1869, every artist achieves a moral influence as well as aesthetic beauty because the work necessarily springs from his whole personality, including his moral nature. The greatest artist does not shape incidents for a conscious moral effect, but this comes naturally if he is writing properly, as a complete man.[2] And the *Saturday Review* in 1874 also traces aesthetic and moral effect back to a common origin, in order to make a plea for greater freedom in art: 'The difference between moral and immoral art is not in the subject-matter, but in the mode of treatment; it is not that one writer deals with bigamy, and another never suggests a breach of the marriage laws; but that one possesses a healthy, and the other a morbid, mind.'[3] Leslie Stephen's whole theory of morality in art is based on this, and can be summed up in a phrase that is also a key to the criticism of so many of his contemporaries: '. . . I measure the worth of a book by the worth of the friend whom it reveals to me.'[4] This idea is constantly repeated, without much concern for the difficulties concealed in it; and even for that criticism which was just beginning to concentrate on the work-in-itself, the author's moral nature remained a useful, and in fact ultimate, criterion. 'The question [of morality]', Henry James wrote around 1907, 'comes back thus, obviously, to the kind and the degree of the artist's prime sensibility, which is the soil out of which his subject springs . . . this enveloping air of the artist's humanity—which gives the last touch to the worth of the work.'[5]

[1] *George Eliot Letters*, ed. G. S. Haight, New Haven, 1954–5, vii, 44.

[2] 'Charles Dickens', *Contemporary Rev.* x (1869), 204–5.

[3] 'Sensationalism', xxxvii (1874), 614–15.

[4] 'The Moral Element in Literature', *Cornhill Mag.* xliii (1881), 41. For more on Stephen's moral theories, see below, pp. 91–92.

[5] Preface to *The Portrait of a Lady*, in *The Art of the Novel*, London, 1935, p. 45. See also 'The Art of Fiction', *Longman's Mag.* iv (1884), 520.

A third approach by critics is to consider the way a novel expresses its values through its treatment of the characters. Generally, this is seen simply as a provision of exempla, good and evil. Good characters are either choice specimens of humanity not often met with, or else are completely transfigured beyond reality. According to the *Contemporary* in 1868, just as history is said to be philosophy teaching through examples, so the novel teaches by even higher examples: that is, by the portrayal of the ideal type.[1] And R. Y. Tyrrell in 1889 regrets that Trollope does not provide us with 'an ideal of human conduct and aspiration': 'There is nothing elevating or even improving in fiction which presents us with characters which are never on a higher or larger scale than ourselves, of a more generous or loftier cast than the persons one meets at a dinner party or in a club smoking-room. The types of character should be presented to us in such a way as to stimulate our imagination, and kindle our admiration and love.'[2]

The comments of one practising novelist on how he moralizes through characters are revealing. Charles Reade, whose hoarse denunciations of critics and Press trouble the first twenty years of the period, continually defends himself from charges of immorality by pointing to his careful treatment of character. For example, in 1866 he defends *Griffith Gaunt*: 'In my double character of moralist and artist . . . I fill my readers with a horror of Bigamy, and a wholesome indignation against my principal male character, so far as I have shown him.'[3] And in 1871 he takes the same attitude to the controversial figures of Sir Charles Bassett and Rhoda Somerset in *A Terrible Temptation*, saying of the former: '. . . I have openly disapproved his early life—have represented him as heartily regretting it, so soon as the virtuous love dawned on him; and yet I have shown some consequences of his early frailties following him for years. If this

[1] vii (1868), 466–7.

[2] 'Mr. Norris's Novels', *Quarterly Rev.* clxviii (1889), 434–5.

[3] 'The Prurient Prude', *Readiana*, 1883, p. 316.

is not fiction teaching morality in its own unobtrusive way—what is?'[1] And of Rhoda Somerset:

Do I whitewash the hussy, or make her a well-bred, delicate-minded woman, as your refined and immoral writers would? I present her illiterate, coarse, vain, with good impulses, a bad temper, and a Billingsgate tongue. In close contrast to this unattractive photograph I am careful to place my portrait of an English virgin, drawn in the sweetest colours my rude art can command, that every honest reader may see on which side my sympathies lie, and be attracted to virtue by the road of comparison.[2]

The slightest confusion in the distribution of good and evil labels—such as the faintly attractive villain or modestly back-sliding hero—is often received with exaggerated dismay. In 1868 the *Athenaeum*, for example, laboriously takes issue with the sympathetic portrayal of a homicidal clergyman, arguing that although his deed might be forgiven in real life, art demands a more clear-cut morality than the everyday:

. . . most persons who feel strongly with respect to the influence and responsibilities of art will agree in thinking that novelists should be no less disinclined to mitigate the blackness of sin than to obscure the brightness of virtue, and that they invite reprehension when they present us with cases of crime so modified by extenuating circumstances that whilst the extenuating circumstances cover the criminal with sympathy and admiration, his evil act rouses no abhorrence.[3]

And Mrs. Craik, in a late but still not untypical example, agrees in 1882 that good characters may have faults in real life, but to show this in fiction is to 'produce a blurred and blotted vision of life, which, to those just beginning life, is either infinitely sad, or infinitely harmful'. To affect readers with sentiment on behalf, say, of some unhappily married person in a novel who falls in love with another is the height of immorality. In such books, 'Instead of white being white, and black, black, both take a sort of neutral tint—the white not so very pure after all, and the black toned down into an aesthetic grey'. This is no way to

[1] 'A Terrible Temptation', ibid. p. 284.

[2] 'Facts Must be Faced', ibid. p. 323.

[3] 1868 (ii), 13–14.

provide youthful readers with the necessary armour for the Battle of Life.[1]

Other accounts try to avoid this simplicity of moral tag in the drawing of characters. For example, an article in the *Westminster* for 1892 praises Hardy for the delicate moral shading that will 'bewilder those accustomed to draw a sharp line between the sheep and the goats'. Yet, like the others, this writer goes on to praise the way in which 'unselfish conduct is pointed out with admiration, and meanness and self-seeking are shown to be unlovely and disastrous'.[2] And once again, the *means* by which this evaluation has been conveyed are left unexamined.

Poetic justice, finally, is recognized by Victorian critics at all times as another device for formulating a view of life; but there is obviously little need felt to re-examine such a time-honoured convention. 'We look in a novel for something that shall satisfy the instinct for poetic justice', says *London Society* in 1869, confident of being understood and approved.[3] One who certainly approved was John Ruskin, a particularly eloquent defender of the device. In letter 83 of *Fors Clavigera*, in 1877, he calls it the highest imaginative expression of the moral law, and the clearest sign of divinity in the works of the masters:

And this so-called poetical justice, asserted by the great designers, consists not only in the gracing of virtue with her own proper rewards of mental peace and spiritual victory; but in the proportioning also of worldly prosperity to visible virtue; and the manifestation, therefore, of the presence of the Father in this world, no less than in that which is to come. So that, if the life-work of any man of unquestioned genius does not assert this visible justice, but, on the contrary, exhibits good and gentle persons in unredeemed distress or destruction,—that work will invariably be found to show no power of design; but to be merely the consecutive collection of interesting circumstances well described, as continually the best work of Balzac, George Sand, and other good novelists of the second order.[4]

[1] *Plain Speaking*, 1882, 177–81.

[2] Janetta Newton-Robinson, 'A Study of Mr. Thomas Hardy', cxxxvii (1892), 157.

[3] 'The Piccadilly Papers', xv (1869), 474.

[4] 1871–84, vii, 355–7.

Inevitably, there is a resurgence of views like Ruskin's when the realists arrive. James, for example, is all the time reproved for showing only the defeat of goodness, instead of those happier 'providences of fiction' which best express the 'moral equitics of life'.[1] For such critics—and they are by far the majority—the romance comes as a deliverer, its independence of real life leaving it perfectly free to embody the higher workings of Providence. According to an enthusiastic Amelia Edwards, the fascination of fiction from the earliest times (she goes back to Egyptian papyri) has always lain in its enshrining poetic justice: 'It satisfies our inborn sense of right; it transports us into a purer atmosphere; it vindicates the ways of God to Man.'[2] And Hall Caine, lastly, makes the convention one of his 'New Watchwords of Fiction' in 1890. The romance, he believes, is the natural vehicle for the moral idealism which always shows ultimate degradation to befall the wicked, even if they should prosper at first. Though endings can be sad they can still be just, and indeed all imaginative art *must* end in justice: 'The incidents of life are only valuable to art in degree as they are subservient to an idea, and an idea is only valuable to man in the degree to which it helps him to see that come what will the world is founded on justice. . . . Justice is the one thing that seems to give art a right to exist, and justice—poetic justice, as we call it—is the essence of Romanticism.'[3]

III. ATTACKS ON DIDACTICISM

Beneath all this pious rhetoric and attachment to moral purpose, however, there flowed an interesting current of unrest in the shape of a hostility to certain forms of didacticism. It was no revolution against morality's place in literature, but an opposition, rather, to certain methods of revealing it. The approach, being suspicious and, on the whole, less naïve, brings some critics a little closer to the problem.

[1] *Spectator*, liv (1881), 185–6 (by R. H. Hutton).

[2] 'The Art of the Novelist', *Contemporary Rev.* lxvi (1894), 225–6.

[3] ibid. lvii (1890), 486–7.

At their most basic, many critiques of this kind merely assert enigmatically that preaching in fiction is bad, but the conveying of moral lessons good. The *British Quarterly*, in the earlier years, is frequently in this dilemma. In one article in 1867, it says that fiction has no business to inculcate a lesson, yet defines the highest kind of novel as one that expounds important truths and exhibits moral earnestness: Scott had no ethical purpose, but fills his readers with truth and instruction.[1] Similarly, the *Saturday Review* praises Turgenev: 'His style is not in the least didactic, but his writings generally convey a useful lesson to his countrymen.'[2] And Walter Besant insists in 1884 that for a novelist to start out with a conscious moral purpose has by now become almost a law of fiction-writing, but that he must avoid preaching.[3]

Even these imprecise warnings—coming as they do from the most morally-conscious sources—show how widespread was the idea that art and instruction were not always in accord. And when critics come to give reasons for their dislike of 'preaching', the awareness of the difference becomes clearer. Among the most obvious complaints are that it is contrary to the pleasure-giving function of the novel, and also to its proper subject-matter. The *Westminster* expresses this succinctly in an attack on the pretentiousness of Lytton in 1865: '. . . a novel ceases to be a novel when it aims at philosophical teaching. It is not the vehicle for conveying knowledge. Its business is to amuse, and give us that insight into human affairs which is obtained by the observation of character.'[4] In the same year, in *Fraser's*, Edward Dowden expresses indignation at the novelist 'who would entice us into listening to his homily under pretence of amusing us; we see the sulphur in that treacle, pah! and will none of it'[5]; and even the *North British Review* (the somewhat unwieldy organ of the Free Church of Scotland) urges the novelist to abandon

[1] 'George Eliot', xlv (1867), 143.

[2] xxiv (1867), 322–3.

[3] *The Art of Fiction*, pp. 24–25.

[4] 'Modern Novelists: Sir Edward Bulwer-Lytton', xxvii, n.s. (1865), 482–3.

[5] 'Fiction and its Uses', lxxii (1865), 759.

high-flown philosophic purpose and to concentrate on reproducing nature and the heart of man.[1]

By the seventies, similar protests are heard everywhere. The *Saturday* in 1871 confesses that to find a novelist being so false to his proper function as to deliver a moral or a political lecture is enough to make the outraged reader adopt the contrary view[2]; and in the following year the didacticism of *Middlemarch* leads to some words on the proper concern of fiction: 'No talent, not genius itself, can quite overcome the inherent defect of a conspicuous, constantly prominent lesson, or bridge over the disparity between the storyteller with an ulterior aim ever before his own eyes and the reader's, and the ideal storyteller whose primary impulse is a story to tell, and human nature to portray—not human nature as supporting a theory, but human nature as he sees it.'[3]

Another common complaint to be expected is that didacticism causes 'unnaturalness'. Both in his character and plot, George MacDonald, for example, finds short shrift from the *Pall Mall Gazette* in 1882: 'They are not personages, but merely, like the figures on the slides of a magic-lantern, illustrations of the author's lecture. They come like shadows, and so depart. And it is much the same with the story. It moves in a shifting, intermittent way, and in a series of crude pictures, one pausing before us till it has served the lecturer's purpose, and then shifted to make room for another.'[4] Ten years later Mrs. Humphry Ward's didacticism comes under the same attack, for its perverting the true aims of fiction, 'the evolution of natural results from a natural plot by natural characters'.[5] And George Gissing in 1900 takes up the complaint that the modern novel of ideas has just the same flaws as the old novels of moral purpose: 'Its common characteristic is a lack of the novelist's prime virtue, the ability

[1] 'German Novelists: Freytag, Auerbach, Heyse', iv, n.s. (1865), 324–5 (by E. Wilberforce).

[2] xxxii (1871), 404–5.

[3] *Saturday Rev.* xxxiv (1872), 733–4.

[4] 'Dr. MacDonald's New Novel', xxxvi (28 October 1882), 4–5.

[5] 'David Grieve', *Edinburgh Rev.* clxxv (1892), 519–20 (by R. E. Prothero).

to create and present convincing personalities. In the argumentative and exhortative novel we are not concerned with persons, but with types.'[1]

If these are the dangers, how is the novel to avoid them? Some means of indirect suggestion is usually implied to be the answer. The *Saturday*, in an obituary of Mrs. Gaskell in 1865, praises her development away from the open didacticism of her earlier works: 'She gained the knowledge that the power of the novelist to impress a lesson lies in the perfection of the art with which the lesson, whatever it may be, is kept out of sight.'[2] And Walter Raleigh in 1897 derides those 'artless readers' who do not see that the moral is an inseparable part of the imagination, expression, and style of a novel.[3]

'Principles in action' is a familiar phrase used to describe the process of dramatization such critics have in mind. If character, plot, scene, symbol, and all the other devices of the novelist are the way he has turned his own inner experience into emblematic 'action', then his values and beliefs must also be made emblematic and 'active'. When he fails to do this, critics are always pointing out, it is the essential unity of the book that suffers. Even the *British Quarterly*, which has jettisoned many of its old pieties by 1880, can condemn the didacticism of Charlotte Yonge and Jean Ingelow for infringing the 'higher unity' of art, which requires that 'the lesson must be suggested and subordinated.'[4] The *Saturday* takes a particularly firm stand on the principle. In 1872, for example, it attacks two novels that have been wrecked by their evident moral purpose: 'A novel with a purpose, to be in any way interesting, ought to be subtle and suggestive rather than direct. It should convey its meaning by character and action rather than by avowed teaching; and because its aim is didactic, care should be taken to keep its method

[1] 'The Coming of the Preacher', *Literature*, vi (1900), 15–16. Typically, Gissing goes on to suggest that this is inevitable in such an era, and is vaguely hopeful that literary value *can* somehow be combined with the spiritual improvement of society.

[2] 'Mrs. Gaskell', xx (1865), 638–9.

[3] *Style*, 1897, p. 83.

[4] lxxi (1880), 521.

dramatic.'[1] In the following year it rebukes Lytton's *The Parisians* for its failure to observe this dramatic criterion and to 'crystallize into artistic form'. Didactic purpose in fiction is only admissible where the author's imagination has been intense enough to fuse his abstract principles into artistic symbols and not to leave them as 'raw masses of sermon . . . interspersed in the middle of story-telling'.[2] And in 1875 the same periodical gives Scott as an example of this successful use of 'symbols' to impress on us, unconsciously and undidactically, certain 'psychological, moral and aesthetic views'.[3]

By this same standard of organic unity, George Eliot is defended by Edward Dowden and (more typical of the general opinion) criticized by Sidney Colvin—an example of how the disagreement of critics over an individual judgment can be less important historically than their agreement on the theoretical principle behind it. Dowden claims that George Eliot is as much an artist as a teacher: 'There is not a hard kernel of dogma at the centre of her art, and around it a sheath or envelope which we break and throw away; the moral significance coalesces with the narrative, and lives through the characters.'[4] And Colvin, writing later with the example of *Daniel Deronda* before him, makes a partly unfavourable comparison with George Sand. In the latter's writings,

> every image is conceived in relation to the whole, nothing comes to jar or distract us. In the work of George Eliot, moral and philosophical problems do not clothe themselves, with the same certainty of instinct, in appropriate artistic forms. We have passages of first-rate art side by side with passages of philosophy; and sometimes the philosophy comes where we want the art, and gives us a character like Daniel Deronda himself, who seems constructed rather than created.[5]

[1] xxxiii (1872), 193–4. [2] xxxvi (1873), 815–16.

[3] 'Novel-Reading as a Vice', xl (1875), 452–3.

[4] 'George Eliot', *Contemporary Rev.* xx (1872), 404.

[5] 'Daniel Deronda', *Fortnightly Rev.* xx, n.s. (1876), 615. Dowden found nothing to make him change his mind when the widely-criticized *Deronda* appeared, and in fact preferred it to *Middlemarch* (' "Middlemarch" and "Daniel Deronda" ', *Contemporary Rev.* xxix, 1876–7, 348–69).

George Saintsbury and Leslie Stephen are two notable—and representative—figures who demand more detailed attention in this matter of didacticism. The former, as befits 'the High Pontiff of Criticism',[1] is continually pronouncing against the inartistic embodiment of values. For example, in the *Academy* (his favourite podium) he uses both George MacDonald's *Malcolm* in 1875 and *Daniel Deronda* in the following year to illustrate 'the immutable law that no perfect novel can ever be written in designed illustration of a theory, whether moral or immoral, and that art, like Atticus and the Turk, will bear no rival near the throne'.[2] And again, in the *Fortnightly* he insists that morality must be regarded as part of the artist's raw material—one factor that regulates men's relations in real life—and not as something added by the author in his capacity of thinker or moral agent: 'The novel has nothing to do with any beliefs, with any convictions, with any thoughts in the strict sense, except as mere garnishings. Its substance must always be life not thought, conduct not belief, the passions not the intellect, manners and morals not creeds and theories.'[3]

However, despite his wavering attachment to art for art's sake in his criticism of poetry, Saintsbury never lost sight of the novelist's special moral responsibility: 'The truth is, that the novel is, while the poem is not, mainly and firstly a criticism of life.'[4] Though extremely liberal for his time, he often reveals his basic kinship to it. For example, his reply to the charge of indelicacy in Gautier is that, though writing for adults, the Frenchman is basically moral: . . . 'his ardent admiration for beauty preserved him from all the uglier faults of immorality, and often led him back to the accepted code, though by a somewhat roundabout way.'[5] And on Feuillet: 'He proceeds distinctly

[1] So called by *The Times Lit. Supp.* 1907, p. 321.

[2] vii (1875), 34; and x (1876), 253–4.

[3] 'The Present State of the Novel. I', *Fortnightly Rev.* xlii, n.s. (1887), 416.

[4] 'The Present State of the English Novel, 1892', *Miscellaneous Essays*, 1892, p. 417. For Saintsbury's Aestheticism, cf. Dorothy Richardson, 'Saintsbury and Art for Art's Sake in England', *P.M.L.A.* lix (1944), 243–60.

[5] 'Théophile Gautier', *Fortnightly Rev.* xxiii, n.s. (1878), 431.

upon the lines of religion and morality . . . and in his descriptions he very carefully avoids undue complaisance and undue luxuriance of language.'[1] But on at least one occasion, in a later essay on Maupassant, Saintsbury manages to escape from his quandary by dismissing immorality *and* didacticism as basically the same thing: an obsession which fetters the artist's imagination, whether it is conventional righteousness, or, in Maupassant's case, materialist pessimism: '[The artist] is to see life whole as far as he can; and it is impossible that he should see it whole if he is under the domination of any 'ism to the extent that Maupassant was under the domination of this.'[2] 'Wholeness of vision' is Saintsbury's standard here—a familiar concept, but one which even modern aestheticians have found useful in searching for a link between artistic and philosophic truth.

Leslie Stephen, similarly, attacks open didacticism while at the same time adopting a firm—even firmer—moral position. Lytton's self-conscious philosophizing, for example, is faulted for the unnaturalness it causes[3]; but the idea of poetic justice in literature—'that a villain is hanged and a good man presented with a thousand pounds'—is twice criticized not just for being inartistic but for being morally improper.[4] The whole of his 'Art and Morality' in 1875 is a defence of the part played by morality in all literature, and is consciously in dispute with what it calls the growing theory that the two inhabit different worlds. He admits that prudery is to be avoided, and above all, as even some great writers have forgotten, preaching: 'That is a blunder in art; but the blunder is not that they moralised, but that they moralised in a wrong way.' The right way is the expression of values through 'vivid imaginative symbols' rather than 'abstract logical formulae'. Fundamentally, as we have seen before, the question for Stephen is one of the soundness of the artist's personality. If art teaches, it is by our being 'put *en rapport* with

[1] 'Octave Feuillet', ibid. xxiv, n.s. (1878), 102.

[2] 'Guy de Maupassant', *National Rev.* xxi (1893), 822–6.

[3] 'The Late Lord Lytton as a Novelist', *Cornhill Mag.* xxvii (1873), 348.

[4] 'Richardson's Novels', ibid. xvii (1868), 52–53; 'Art and Morality', ibid. xxxii (1875), 101.

a great and good man'.[1] And if there is to be an acceptable 'purpose' in a novel, it must be instinctive in the artist and consistent with his spontaneity, so as to maintain the unified personality which is the secret of creativity and the final criterion of worth.[2]

To connect in this way the moral issue with the nature of the artist's imagination is to hint at a fairly comprehensive theory. It is similar to Saintsbury's, though more clearly developed. Stephen's belief can be seen at work in the 1868 essay on Richardson, where he concedes that the novelist's moral earnestness in this case, for all the artistic flaws that result from it, has the one great advantage that it has become part of his imagination, 'and leads to a certain intensity of realization which we are apt to miss in the novelist's without a purpose'.[3] The later George Eliot, he writes in 1902, is an example of someone who fails at times to achieve this fusion of the imaginative and the reflective faculties: the enforcement of a moral maxim too easily destroys 'the spontaneity which marks a true imaginative inspiration'. But on the other hand, a writer can never ignore the beliefs that have shaped 'his own microcosm'; and although Stephen is inclined to suggest that certain beliefs are more suitable for the writer's microcosm than others—a code embodying 'the chivalrous and manly virtues'—his outlook is preserved from moral absolutism by always returning to the nature of the artist: 'It does not matter so much why a writer should be profoundly interested in his work, nor to what use he may intend to apply it, as that, somehow or other, his interest should be aroused, and the world which he creates be a really living world for his imagination.'[4] His ideas, though they never evolve into full theory, are based on some implied region of the creative process where artistic imagination and philosophic values coalesce—a mental region where the greatest works are forged, and where the problem of didacticism ceases to exist.

[1] *Cornhill Mag.* xxxii (1875), 91–101. See above, p. 81.

[2] 'The Moral Element in Literature', ibid. xliii (1881), 34–50.

[3] 'Richardson's Novels', ibid. xvii (1868), 53.

[4] *George Eliot* (English Men of Letters Series), 1902, pp. 112–18.

IV. THE NINETIES

When the nineties are reached, some radical change might have been expected in the moral aspects of novel-theory. But in spite of Wilde's dictum, 'There is no such thing as a moral or an immoral book. Books are well written, or badly written. That is all',[1] late-Victorian critics of the novel were remarkably unaffected by the ideas of Aestheticism, and the moral-utilitarian strain in English thought still predominated.[2] For example, in a heated controversy over art and morality in the correspondence columns of the *Scots Observer* in 1890, Charles Whibley is one of the few contributors not to toe the traditionalist line with reference to the novel. He makes an interesting Pateresque attempt to explain the flaws of such 'improper' works as Maupassant's *Bel-Ami* and Daudet's *Sapho* in terms of form alone, denying the relevance of the moral objection and insisting that faulty treatment and 'lack of proportion' are the only possible basis of condemnation. When tried against the criterion of harmony, or arrangement, or selection, Dostoevsky, often criticized on moral grounds, is totally exculpated, and 'has justified by his grandeur of treatment the selection of hideous types and squalid incidents'; while Wilde's *Dorian Gray* is to be criticized not for 'immorality', which is meaningless, but for a disproportion in style.[3]

Such an account as Whibley's is almost unique. What is more generally noticeable is not a growing demand for the novel's independence of morality but the familiar one for an end to prudery. W. E. Henley, for example, is one of the loudest opponents of restrictions on art. His defence of Maupassant is liberal

[1] 'A Preface to "Dorian Gray" ', *Fortnightly Rev.* xlix, n.s. (1891), 480–1. Elsewhere, Wilde gives a more conservative account of the place of morals in fiction ('Balzac in English', *Pall Mall Gazette*, xliv, 13 September 1886, 5).

[2] An account laying more emphasis on the novel's movement towards Aestheticism and less on the conservatism of critics can be found in Louise Rosenblatt, *L'Idée de l'art pour l'art dans la littérature anglaise*, Paris, 1931, pp. 207–41.

[3] iv (1890), 226–7. Whibley expands this attack on the 'confusion of literature with its material' in *Studies in Frankness*, 1898, pp. 1–25.

BIRKBECK LIBRARY

in the extreme, claiming that the great realist's limitations are technical, not moral: '. . . the merit of a book is neither lessened nor enhanced by the morals of its hero; and when you begin to apply to art the standards of life, from that moment your criticism becomes worthless and impertinent. A novelist is neither a preacher nor a policeman.' Yet Henley goes on to draw the line at *Bel-Ami* on the grounds that it is 'written from a sheer love of caddishness'[1]; and through all of his criticism, behind the assaults on conventional morality and the proclamations of artistic freedom, is a firmly-held 'activist' ethic, a mixture of Ruskin and Outward Bound.[2]

Perhaps even more typical of the iconoclasts of the nineties is Havelock Ellis, who, like Henley, never dismisses the relevance of morality even though he is one of the main pioneers in the expansion of the novel's frontiers. His plea is simply and continually that this morality should not be the Juggernaut of Grundyism. In 1896 he writes that Zola is to be praised for increasing the realm of experience open to the novel, and that the groundless charges of immorality brought against *Jude the Obscure* are simply those that could be made against every great novel. The novelist, he admits, cannot be said to have nothing to do with morals, because the human passions that are his material are at their most profound when in conflict with traditional morality: '. . . his art lies in drawing the sinuous woof of human nature between the rigid warp of morals.' But the only obligation he faces in his treatment of this material (and Ellis echoes Saintsbury and Stephen) is that he should never be dominated by *any* purpose, either moral or immoral: 'An artist's private opinions concerning the things that are good and bad in the larger world are sufficiently implicit in the structure of his own smaller world; the counsel that he should make them explicit in a code of rules and regulations for humanity at large is a

[1] 'Modern Men. Guy de Maupassant', *Scots Observer*, iv (1890), 582–3 (attributed to Henley in M. U. Schappes, 'William Ernest Henley's Principles of Criticism', *P.M.L.A.* xlvi, 1931, 1294).

[2] See above, p. 52n.; and J. H. Buckley, *William Ernest Henley*, Princeton, 1945, pp. 162–80.

counsel which, as every artist knows, can only come from the Evil One.'[1]

Many other voices are raised along with Havelock Ellis's. D. F. Hannigan's is shriller, and his lack of argument or balance is overshadowed by the remarkable fact of such opinions appearing in the *Westminster Review* at all: controversial works like *Tess of the D'Urbervilles*, *Jude the Obscure*, *Esther Waters*, and Grant Allen's *The Woman Who Did* are all lauded to the skies, and the freedom of art flaunted in the eyes of the Puritans.[2] More and more praise is accorded to Zola for the liberation and greater seriousness his naturalism has brought to fiction: 'It has cleared the air of a thousand follies, has pricked a whole fleet of oratorical bubbles. . . . The public has eaten of the apple of knowledge, and will not be satisfied with mere marionettes.'[3] And even pessimism and a sense of tragic futility come to be praised, in the case of Flaubert, as being in keeping with the mood of the time and a characteristic of all great artists.[4]

All of this represented an advance, no doubt. The nineties confirmed in an important way the emancipation of the novel which Moore, Hardy, and others had already begun. But as regards the moral theory of fiction, there had been little change. Even the most liberal critics would hardly have gone beyond Stevenson's question-begging cry: 'There is no quite good book without a good morality; but the world is wide, and so are morals.'[5] The disappointingly tentative nature of this aspect of

[1] 'Zola: the Man and his Work', *Savoy*, i (1896), 78; and 'Concerning Jude the Obscure', ibid. iii (1896), 42–49.

[2] 'The Latest Development of English Fiction', cxxxviii (1892), 655–9; 'Sex in Fiction', cxliii (1895), 616–25; and 'Mr. Thomas Hardy's Latest Novel', cxlv (1896), 136–9.

[3] Edmund Gosse, 'The Limits of Realism in Fiction' (1890), in *Questions at Issue*, 1893, pp. 152–3. W. C. Frierson, pointing out that Gosse significantly published his article in America first, sees 1893 as the 'pivotal year' in the battle for realism against prudery in England ('The English Controversy Over Realism in Fiction, 1885–1895', *P.M.L.A.* xliii, 1928, 545).

[4] Ernest Newman, 'Gustave Flaubert', *Fortnightly Rev.* lviii, n.s. (1895), 826–8.

[5] 'A Gossip on a Novel of Dumas's', *Memories and Portraits*, 1887, p. 238.

Victorian criticism cannot be denied. But its value is not determined simply by whether or not it 'solved' the problem of where philosophy and morality connect with art. Many of the critics showed a perturbed awareness of the problem's complexity, a variety in their responses to it, and worked out certain important preliminary steps in its investigation. And in an age obsessed above all by the breakdown of the old philosophies and moralities themselves, perhaps this was an achievement not to be despised.

4

THE TECHNIQUE OF THE NOVEL

THE idea that the novel, like any art, has a technique did not spring full-blown from the head of Jove—or of James. Miriam Allott's belief that Victorian criticism was interested only in verisimilitude, morality, and correctness of style, and that 'the conception of artistic structure' belongs exclusively to the years after Percy Lubbock, is hardly justified even for an earlier period of the nineteenth century, as Richard Stang has shown, and it is certainly not true for the years after 1865.[1] A concern for workmanship and form can be found everywhere, from the short notice in the weekly to the mammoth review-article in the quarterly. There is always a risk of over-emphasizing, through hindsight, the 'modern' tendencies in such criticism; but even when viewed with caution, the Victorian critics of fiction were simply too voluble in their awareness of craft to be ignored or disparaged.

I. PLOT VERSUS CHARACTER: THE FIRST PHASE

The relation between 'character' and 'action' is an ancient debating-point in the theory of drama and epic; and it was appropriate that the novel, as the offspring of both, should inherit the dispute. The long wrangling that ensued over which is superior, character or plot, provides one of the most lively currents in Victorian discussion of technique.

The dominance of the first, due to a new interest in human motives and psychology, has often been said to typify mid- and late-Victorian thinking about the novel, and through the

[1] Miriam Allott, *Novelists on the Novel*, 1959, pp. 162–3; Richard Stang, op. cit. pp. 91–135.

sixties and seventies this is so. As the melodrama of earlier Victorian fiction is superseded by the greater psychological realism of George Eliot and Trollope, critics come to identify 'plot' with the particular incidents and conventions used by older writers. Keningale Cook in 1872, for example, gives some disparaging praise to Fenimore Cooper for being a pioneer in the art of fiction. His impossibly entangled plots, without any depth or delicacy of character-drawing, are recommended ironically as a model for study by the anachronistic sensation-writers of the present day; but since 'the novelist's function is the creation of a prose drama where characters are a primary object, he can scarcely be said to have entered upon art at all in any high sense'.[1]

Wilkie Collins becomes a symbol of the old régime, and at times a martyr to the change in critical taste. His plots are constantly derided as 'Chinese puzzles', and the *Athenaeum*, typically, criticizes his naïve psychology and lack of 'analysis of human nature' in 1872: 'Mr. Wilkie Collins is a very clever mechanist, and a very inferior novelist.'[2] The *Westminster* denies that any high merit resides in *Armadale* having an ingenious plot, which should always be considered merely as a frame to the picture of characters[3]; and R. F. Littledale, in the *Academy*, uses Collins as the very touchstone of this kind of literary inferiority: '. . . the art of constructing plots, where there is any genuine literary faculty, becomes after a time a pure matter of knack, altogether inferior in value and interest, as Mr. Wilkie Collins has satisfactorily established, to the power of drawing character or writing good conversation.'[4] Uncomfortably aware of his reputation, Collins always insisted that the creation of character was a major concern in his writing. In the 1861 Preface to *The Woman in White* he attempts to show how 'story', although a novelist's first object, is dependent on the interest of its characters: 'It may be possible, in novel-writing,

[1] 'American Novelists. 1. James Fenimore Cooper', *Belgravia*, xviii (1872), 386.

[2] 1872 (i), 202–3. [3] xxx, n.s. (1866), 269–71. [4] viii (1875), 216.

to present characters successfully without telling a story; but it is not possible to tell a story successfully without presenting characters: their existence, as recognisable realities, being the sole condition on which the story can be effectively told.'[1] And by 1883, when his brand of plot-interest was even more outmoded, he addresses his readers, half-complaining, half-reassuring, to the effect that their misguided preference for the plotless novel of character and humour will be satisfied in *Heart and Science* by his deliberate attempt to meet their wants.[2]

Apart from its lack of modernity, another objection to plot at this time is that it necessarily appeals to inferior faculties in the reader, compared with the imaginative power needed to follow human motives. The *Saturday* in 1874 claims that the obviousness of this answers the question of the relative merits of plot and character:

A combination of intricate convolutions of circumstance, a series of traps set by fate to which men and women play puppets, may excite a breathless excitement once; but there is no depth of interest in it. When its impression has once been conveyed to the mind, no further interest or excitement can be derived from it. When characters, on the other hand, are depicted skilfully and forcibly, the attention aroused by the book wherein they have their being is of a more permanent if of a less violent kind. There is a more vital interest in the natures than in the circumstances of men.[3]

More significantly, perhaps, concentration on plot is also regarded as endangering the all-important 'naturalness' of character. The *Saturday*, admitting, as do so many, the superior skill of the French in plot and construction, also notes the sacrifice of character which this entails. In the case of Balzac and Hugo, the figures are forced into unreal postures by the need for effect; whereas the greater digressiveness of English novelists has at least the merits of allowing scope in which to develop the characters.[4] And the *Eclectic*, in its bombardment of Miss Braddon, attributes the falsity of her characters to their

[1] 1861 edn., p. viii.
[2] Preface, pp. vii–ix.
[3] xxxviii (1874), 774-5.
[4] 'French Novels', xxi (1866), 615-16.

'having been made to meet the requirements of the story; they are themselves evolved from it, and not the story from them'.[1]

As well as distorting character, plot is also felt to be inferior through its own intrinsic unnaturalness. The *Westminster* in 1876 places it third of the three components of fiction, after character (the 'all-ruling element') and scenery: 'While character and scenery may be said to unfold a mystery, it is the purpose of the plot to create one. It is the most artificial portion of the work, and, therefore, the furthest removed from nature.'[2] And *Tinsley's Magazine* in the following year maintains that in serious novels 'a plot is certainly not necessary to artistic perfection', because no genuine plot or pattern can be detected in ordinary human lives, except at a level too deep for the ordinary novelist. When a pattern is imposed, artificiality and convention are bound to result.[3]

The argument, however, was not wholly one-sided. Even during these earlier years, when the reaction against an older kind of novel was at its height, the new preference for character did not blind all critics to the value of a contrived pattern of incidents and situations. Dallas's *The Gay Science* (1866) contains a brief and very unusual defence of the 'Novel of Plot' on the grounds that it is consistent with the contemporary decline of the hero. The inevitable impression it gives of man as a puppet of circumstance, he suggests, is at least as justified as the idea, in the 'Novel of Character', that man moulds his own fate. The flaw of sensation novels is not that they belong to one type rather than the other, but that they mix the genres, inserting into a novel of plot one central heroic figure from the other tradition.[4] More typical of the favourable view of plot, however, is a *British Quarterly* review in 1871 which calls the story the novel-writer's first concern, like composition in a painting, and urges an author to create an evolving movement and a

[1] 'Miss Braddon. The Illuminated Newgate Calendar', xiv, n.s. (1868), 32–33.

[2] 'Ouida's Novels', xlix, n.s. (1876), 363.

[3] 'Novel-writing as an Art', xx (1877), 329.

[4] ii, 292–5.

structure tight enough to sustain the characters.[1] The *Spectator* in 1875 declares that 'one of the first qualifications of a novelist is to understand the art of telling a story', and that without this art, which is as essential as colour to a painter, a novel cannot wholly succeed, even if it contains 'subtle delineations of character, exquisite descriptive passages, pregnant thoughts, and witty dialogue'.[2] And G. H. Lewes in 1865 takes the same view of priorities: 'The distinctive element in Fiction is that of plot-interest. The rest is vehicle.'[3] But as Lewes makes clear, and as is implicit in many other such statements, to recognize the primacy of story-telling among the technical skills of the novelist is far from according it primacy among the 'higher interests' by which literature is judged.

Behind this opposing of plot to character, which is at its most abrupt before 1875, there lies an assumption that the two are somehow detachable. And most critics, like Trollope, see the former as ancillary, a framework for the realistic portrait-gallery which is the true end of fiction.[4] There is little attempt to look more closely at the relation between the two: at most, it is urged that action should 'proceed' or 'evolve' out of character, although this is usually just a way of expressing the greater value of the latter. One example, however, is outstanding—a review of W. G. Wills's *The Three Watches*, in the *Spectator* for 1865, which gives a more interesting picture of the relationship than most, in its account of the effect upon plot of inferior characterization:

Perhaps it is on the progress of the story itself that the want of graduation in the conceptions, the want of the finer shades, the absence of reflected lights, the singleness, or at most duality of attitude in all the characters tells most injuriously. The result is that the story moves on by fits and starts rather than continuously, and the *dénouement* is arrived at almost unfairly by a sharp and almost treacherous rebound from the previously indicated ending. The cause

[1] liv (1871), 546. [2] xlviii (1875), 407–9 (by John Dennis).

[3] 'Criticism in Relation to Novels', *Fortnightly Rev.* iii (1865–6), 354.

[4] *An Autobiography*, 1883, i, 169–70 (Chapter 7).

probably is that there is no preparation for movement in the characters, no subtleties which change of circumstances is wanted to bring out. For the most part the circumstances change alone, without developing new aspects in the actors. The result is that the joints in the story are almost as awkward as the public shifting of scenes in the theatre. The side-views of character contribute materially to the easy development and graduations of a story; and Mr. Wills gives no side-views of character.[1]

II. THE 'INNER LIFE'

Around 1880 the plot-character controversy enters quite dramatically into a new phase, when the technique of 'analysis' (simply, any detailed examination of personality and motive) comes under violent attack. And it is remarkable how once again the novels of James and Howells (rather than their criticism, which had less immediate influence) act as a catalyst to critical discussion, and in this case as a sign for revolt.

Up till this time the picture had been quite different, and 'analysis', if ever it was recognized as such, enjoyed a great deal of favour. There were a few suspicions of the method at its extreme, of course, particularly when in the hands of the unscrupulous foreigner: 'The English novelist sketches living and self-determining persons; the French novelist either creates an ideal being or dissects some shuddering human specimen, whom he holds, soul and body, at the mercy of his sharp and torturing pen.'[2] The criticism clearly arises from the theory of 'living' characters; and accordingly, there is a widespread feeling that the novelist must show respect for his creatures and not intrude too far on the privacy of their 'inner' being. But as yet, in the earlier years, most native writers did not seem to infringe this law, and most critics freely recommended psychological analysis. Leslie Stephen in 1868, for example, saw Defoe's lack of it as a weakness of imaginative creativity[3]; and

[1] xxxviii (1865), 17–18 (Dr. R. H. Tener attributes this to R. H. Hutton).

[2] 'Middlemarch: a Study of Provincial Life', *Quarterly Rev.* cxxxiv (1873), 359 (by R. Laing).

[3] 'De Foe's Novels', *Cornhill Mag.* xvii (1868), 302–3.

the *Athenaeum*, reviewing *The Claverings* in the previous year, makes a not uncommon criticism of Trollope, that he 'omits all the psychology, and merely touches the external appearances'—though adding enigmatically that with such 'deeper studies in human nature' the book 'might not have been so pleasant to read'.[1] Other critics hail the technique as an advance in the art of fiction, and the most significant feature of modern writing. In 1873 the *London Quarterly* suggest that the mark of the really modern novelist is to describe the hidden springs of action, the inner mystery of the human consciousness, rather than man in society.[2] And George Eliot is particularly admired on this account, 'H. Lawrenny' (Edith Simcox) ascribing historical importance to *Middlemarch*:

> *Middlemarch* marks an epoch in the history of fiction in so far as its incidents are taken from the inner life, as the action is developed by the direct influence of mind on mind and character on character, as the material circumstances of the outer world are made subordinate and accessory to the artistic presentation of a definite passage of mental experience, but chiefly as giving a background of perfect realistic truth to a profoundly imaginative psychological study.[3]

Even James's methods of characterization received some cautious approval at first. The *British Quarterly*, in spite of its distaste for his 'painfulness', bravely admires the power of his 'rare faculty of moral analysis, his keen penetration of moral causes' in *Roderick Hudson*.[4] And the *Athenaeum*, unaware of the nettle in its grasp, prefaces a quiet notice of *Daisy Miller* with another review in which superficial characterization is criticized: 'From one who has the capacity of writing, to begin with, the present generation requires more than mere word painting; it wants the analysis of thought and motive. One of the highest modes of fiction is divination, and those who appear capable of wielding the rod must be urged to do it.'[5]

[1] 1867 (i), 1783.
[2] 'The Writings of Berthold Auerbach', xxix (1873), 344.
[3] *Academy*, iv (1873), 1–4.
[4] lxx (1879), 529–30.
[5] 1879 (i), 275–6.

The change, when it came, was drastic, and surprisingly sudden. Within the space of a few years, 'analysis' acquires various new and unpleasant associations, and the periodicals of the eighties are filled with angry abuse. The most common charge is that the latest novelists have mistakenly adopted the heartless methods of science. Julia Wedgwood waxes virulent over *The Bostonians* in 1886, and calls its revelation of characters 'a violation of every conceivable rule of literary good breeding': 'The mistake is a result of that obsequious deference which Literature has in these days shown to triumphant Science; an instance of that obliteration of all reserve which the new lawgiver demands and she abhors.'[1]

The idea is constantly expressed in such scientific images as anatomy and vivisection: 'Human character is to this Paganism as the rapidly decomposing corpse under the knife and microscope.'[2] And it becomes clear that the basis of the hostility is not just the belief in 'living' characters, but a more general preference for the intuitive, rather than the intellectual faculties. Karl Hillebrand, for example, claims in 1884 that only by an intuitive *impression* can one man (or reader) grasp the whole of another man's (or character's) personality. None of the so-called psychological qualities which the analyser enumerates really exist in themselves, but are only intellectual abstractions. Art convinces by producing a disposition in its audience, whereas science produces knowledge: 'True art cares little about the genesis of character; it introduces man as a finished being, and lets him explain himself by his acts and words.'[3] And because of their appeal to the wrong faculties, *Temple Bar* in the same year detects in James and Howells the death-knell of the modern novel:

'Will the reader be content to accept a novel which is an analytic study rather than a story?' We answer emphatically, no. The first

[1] *Contemporary Rev.* l (1886), 300–1.

[2] Maxwell Gray (i.e. Mary Gleed Tuttiett), 'On the Development of Character in Fiction', in *On the Art of Writing Fiction* (by W. E. Norris and others), 1894, pp. 69–72.

[3] 'About Old and New Novels', *Contemporary Rev.* xlv (1884), 392–5.

function of the novel is pleasurably to engage the attention. Its truths must be conveyed to us by means not only of the intellect but the emotions. There are certain finer ethical points which can be understood emotionally as they never could be understood intellectually.

The skilful manipulation of emotional and intellectual machinery, so that one shall help and perfect the other, is the highest triumph of the novelist's art.[1]

Another victim of the reaction was Meredith. For example, in 1886 W. L. Courtney regrets the growth of his analytic power, and the over-refined public taste that favours it (Meredith would have been wryly amused at the idea of an encouraging public). The talent for analysis in a novelist, he holds, is unspontaneous, introverted, and destructive, and is inevitably accompanied by cynicism. Synthesis and an appeal to the heart are the true marks of the artist, and analysis is by definition opposed to both: '. . . the joy of living expires in the sustained effort to disclose the springs on which it depends.'[2] And similarly, W. F. Barry, in the *Quarterly* for 1891, condemns his 'motive-grinding' as fatal to art, which ought to be 'simple, sensuous, and direct', based on the heart rather than the head, and on recognition of the fact that life itself is beyond analysis.[3]

At times it is Stendhal who is seen as the first great transgressor. Arthur Symons regrets in 1899 that the modern novel should have followed his example rather than that of Balzac, who respected the 'life' of his creations and left much of their natures secret—not, like so many novelists since, murdering in order to dissect.[4] But in contrast, Vernon Lee gives the name of 'the School of Stendhal' to those who are opposed to exaggerated analysis, and names Tolstoi as its most prominent member. The Russian's method of sympathy and spontaneity, catching the very vagueness of life, is compared with the false definiteness of the analytical school, who do not write about people as

[1] 'The New School of American Fiction', lxx (1884), 389.

[2] 'George Meredith's Novels', *Fortnightly Rev.* xxxix, n.s. (1886), 771–2.

[3] 'English Realism and Romance', clxxiii (1891), 473–6.

[4] 'Balzac', *Fortnightly Rev.* lxv, n.s. (1899), 753–5.

they *affect* them, but in such a way as to present the neatest diagram. The novel should not give us knowledge of the individual but love, through the intuitions, and an awareness of the *mystery* of other people. Unlike Natasha, Levin, or Julien Sorel, we understand Madame Bovary and Cousine Bette too well. For the novelist to lay bare the soul of his heroine is to convey pain to the reader, and turn 'the poor girl into a sort of walking physiologico-psychologic demonstration'.[1]

Some critics are torn between distaste for the 'morbidity' of the method and their admiration for what it can achieve. The *Westminster* in 1887 tries to resolve this in terms of a racial difference. It declares that the introspection which Howells's analytic method produces in the characters is acceptable only if they are American—in Englishmen it would be unhealthy.[2] And the same magazine is still unable to make up its mind three years later, in a review of Paul Bourget (a writer often linked with the Americans in this respect): 'We have no liking for analytical fiction in general; to us it seems painful and unwholesome—not fulfilling the best function of fiction, which is to take one out of oneself, but, on the contrary, leading to morbid introspection. But, as we have often said before, every style is good when at its best; and analysis in the hands of M. Paul Bourget is at its best.'[3]

A final objection against analysis is that the method is 'over-elaborate', a perverse exaggeration of a minor technique into an end in itself—or worse. Thus, the *Athenaeum*, like most others, finds *The Bostonians* tedious, and its material too flimsy for its method: '. . . he has to fill page after page with long analysis of feelings, or minute descriptions, whether of character or scenery,

[1] 'Rosny and the French Analytical Novel', *Cosmopolis*, vii (1897), 674–87. See also below, p. 138. Much of this attitude, even if not as persuasively expressed as by Vernon Lee, anticipates the recent changes in modern criticism already mentioned (see above, p. 25n.). John Bayley again, for example, echoes Vernon Lee quite closely in his comparison of Tolstoi with the over-systematized presentation of consciousness in Joyce and Faulkner (*The Characters of Love*, 1960, pp. 3–47).

[2] cxxviii (1887), 262.

[3] cxxxiv (1890), 693.

which, subtle and delicate as they often are, produce at last in the reader's mind the same kind of irritation as results from an over-elaborated picture of a subject which might be sufficiently indicated by a few bold strokes.'[1] In 1887, also in the *Athenaeum*'s eyes, Howells 'seems to invert the proper method by setting to work to analyze before he has got the matter to work on'.[2] And in the following year, Saintsbury's fulminations at the analytic method—'which the New World has sent with the Colorado beetle, and the phylloxera, and a hundred other plagues, to punish the rashness of Columbus'—lead him to take the point further. Analysis, he says, is the elaboration not even of a minor technique, but of an activity foreign to art in the first place. Zolaism gives us dry bread, but the Americans give us mere dough:

The analyst . . . is in this worse off than the naturalist pure and simple, that instead of mistaking a partial for a universal method, he takes for a complete method what is not strictly a method at all. The painful copying of an actual scene or action sometimes results in something that is at least an integral part of a story. The elaborate dissection of motives and characters can only result in something that stops short of being even part of a story—that is only preliminary to part of a story.[3]

III. THE RETURN TO PLOT

As part of the reaction against analysis in the eighties, came a resurgence of interest in 'plot' and 'incident'. Even before this time some critics had warned novelists against forgetting the action in their new preoccupation with character. The *Saturday* criticizes a novel in 1872:

There is no careful leading up to that climax; no gradual deepening of the colours, or further entanglement of the threads; no well-graduated *crescendo* passages preparatory to the final burst. It is all on the one string; repetition, not increment or growth. . . . Nothing

[1] 1886 (i), 323. [2] 1887 (ii), 671–2.

[3] 'The Present State of the Novel. II', *Fortnightly Rev.* xliii, n.s. (1888), 116–18.

is more interesting, if well done, than a psychological novel of careful analysis; but then it must be well done, and it must give the reader the impression of growth.[1]

And in 1878 it disapproves of the fact that the fashion among young writers is for the analysis of character at the expense of 'carefully thought out and well developed story'.[2]

The storm broke around Howells's famous essay on James in 1882. This laid down the principle of the new American school as the abandonment of 'the moving accident' in favour of 'the operation of lighter but not really less vital motives'—'an analytic study rather than a story'—and combined it with an attitude to the classical English writers that could not fail to draw the fury of conservative and patriotic critics.[3] As might be expected, the *Quarterly* is in the van of the attack in 1883, with the banner of Sir Walter nailed to the masthead and pouring scorn on any writing 'based upon the principle that the best novelist is he who has no story to tell'. The result, as in *Portrait of a Lady* and *A Modern Instance*, is the apotheosis of dullness, due to the lack of the regularly developing incident and 'conclusiveness' of characters' fates which constitute 'plot': 'There is to be no beginning, no middle, and no end. It is like a lucky-bag at a bazaar—you thrust your hand in anywhere and take out anything you can find.'[4]

Arthur Tilley, in the *National Review* in the same year, professes to disagree with much in the *Quarterly*'s attack; but his more moderate disapproval is based on the same points. He sympathizes with the generality of English readers who insist that a novel must be 'rounded'—that is, that the future destinies of the characters are made known at the end—and that its narrative 'goes forward' without dawdling, both of which conditions the new school fails to fulfil: 'For we all have what Mr. James calls "a weakness for a plot"; which the wise novelist will

[1] xxxiii (1872), 348–9. [2] 'Modern Novels', xlv (1878), 619–20.

[3] 'Henry James, Jr.', *Century Illustr. Monthly Mag.* New York, iii, n.s. (1882–3), 25–29.

[4] 'American Novels', clv (1883), 201–29 (by L. J. Jennings).

humour if he can.' The Americans have great merits, but they break down through their concentration on uncreative analysis and their self-destroying contempt for the 'time-honoured machinery' of catastrophe and accident.[1]

Reviewers everywhere seized on any evidence of plot-contrivance or 'strong situations' in a novel to hold it up as an example of heroic resistance to the foreign invasion. And not surprisingly, many found what they were seeking in the new romance. In fact, the re-emergence of this form owed a great deal to the fact that critical opinion was more than a little disillusioned by what the 'character' novel had become. The first two important statements of the romance's aims, Stevenson's 'A Gossip on Romance' and 'A Humble Remonstrance', come at the height of the attack on analysis, in 1882 and 1884 respectively, and clearly mark the confrontation of two totally opposed tendencies of fiction. In the former, Stevenson regrets that the taste of contemporary writers should be against the novel of incident, since this form woos the reader out and gives him a greater sense of identification with life than the more objective response he feels to character-studies. The striking and passion-filled scene, the incident embodying a crisis, are the very centre of art.[2] 'A Humble Remonstrance', taking its point of departure from James's recent credo in 'The Art of Fiction', distinguishes between the Jamesian 'novel of character', Stevenson's own 'novel of adventure', and the 'dramatic novel'. In the latter two, 'nice portraiture is not required; and we are content to accept mere abstract types, so they be strongly and sincerely moved.' He goes on to claim that 'The novel of character . . . requires no coherency of plot', and that, though its characters are embodied in incident, 'the incidents themselves, being tributary, need not march in a progression'.[3] On the definition of 'incidents' and 'progression' alone—both of which James would as strongly claim to be on his side—the two schools are a world apart.

[1] 'The New School of Fiction', i (1883), 257–68.

[2] *Longman's Mag.* i (1882–3), 69–79.

[3] ibid. v (1884–5), 143–6.

The *Saturday* in 1882 sides with Stevenson's 'Gossip' in deploring the absence of incident in contemporary fiction, and sees a challenge to combat in Howells's essay, in which the New World snaps its fingers at the Old.[1] In the same issue, the *Arabian Nights* is cited to crush the American's claim that there is little value in pure incident and complication:

There is room, of course, for analysis, for study of character, and such studies if excellent will aways find an audience, though not a really popular audience. A 'penny dreadful', ideally speaking, has more that satisfies the deathless human thirst for a story than the most subtle exposition of every half shade of dubious emotion in the mind of an American 'young girl', like 'Dr. Breen'. It would be ruinous to the art of fiction if the opposite theory ever became commonly held by novelists.[2]

And the *Westminster* for 1887, in its enthusiasm at Hall Caine's revival of 'plot' in English fiction, hopefully bids farewell to the 'long-spun mental anatomizing' first instigated by George Eliot.[3]

The same attitude prevailed in the nineties, and partially explained the dislodgement of George Eliot from her pedestal during this decade. T. E. Kebbel, for example, beats her with the well-used stick of Walter Scott for giving us 'diffuse moral analysis' instead of the primary interests of any novel, plot and action—'the rapid movement, the quick sequence of cause and effect'.[4] But the hostility to 'plotlessness' in general never quite approached the urgency of the mid eighties, largely because James was less on the scene, and Howells, amid general plaudits, was evidently returning to the fold. The *Spectator* condemns James's *Terminations* in 1895 for the familiar reasons that it lacks 'a natural movement of incident' and 'violates all the natural traditions of narrative art'[5]; but in 1890 Howells's *A Hazard of New Fortunes* is praised for marking its author's

[1] 'The Modern Novel', liv (1882), 633–4. [2] p. 609.

[3] 'A New Novelist', cxxviii (1887), 840–1.

[4] 'The Waverley Novels', *Quarterly Rev.* clxxx (1895), 454–6.

[5] lxxv (1895), 405–6 (by J. A. Noble).

progress away from his early analytic essays in virtuosity, which his admirers had wrongly erected into something more permanent. His latest phase shows a return to traditional qualities, and is characterized by 'the very thing which the youthful critics treated with lofty contempt as a vulgar sop to the Philistine Cerberus,—an orderly narrative movement towards a definite goal or *dénouement*'.[1]

It might be wondered whether there were no critics at all who favoured the new analytic technique, or who suspected that James's method relied as much on suggestion as vivisection. Surprisingly, there were almost none, even by the nineties. There is unstinted praise for the cleverness and subtlety of these writers, but in most instances some radical qualification follows—and subtlety seems to be used as a mere synonym for cleverness. The later Howells, of course, is a safer subject for the critics who admire analysis-within-limits, and several accept that he has defined the 'novel of the future' by jettisoning the stock-in-trade of incidents and dramatic situations, and by ignoring the ancient superstition among English readers that 'the story's the thing'.[2] But much of this praise for his lack of plot is simply a throwback to the older linking of plot with melodrama, rather than a revolutionary acceptance of his earlier work and theories.

James, whose development was the reverse of Howells's, received little criticism that gave any insight into his methods of characterization and narrative. Even Lena Milman's laudatory article in the *Yellow Book* concedes that his method is too analytical for anything larger than the short story, in which he excels.[3] The *Academy*'s unreserved praise for the nuances of *The Awkward Age* is all the more remarkable by its rarity: '. . . holding aloof as he does, yet without affectation of prudery, from the frank image of an act-in-itself, and dwelling with the

[1] *Spectator*, lxiv (1890), 342–3 (by J. A. Noble).

[2] e.g. *Academy*, xxxvii (1890), 147; and 'A Great American Novel', *Pall Mall Gazette*, xlii (11 September 1885), 5.

[3] 'A Few Notes Upon Mr. James', vii (1895), 72.

thought behind it, he presents a more significant idea of both thinker and doer than were otherwise to be obtained.'[1]

Quite unexpectedly, a hint comes early from James Ashcroft Noble, one of the most conservative of critics, that a new idea of character and plot might underlie the strangeness of James's work, as in the case of *The Portrait of a Lady* in 1881: '. . . nothing in this book or in its predecessors is more remarkable than the masterly painting of moral and intellectual atmosphere—the realisable rendering not of character itself, but of those impalpable radiations of character from which we apprehend it long before we have *data* that enable us fully to comprehend it.'[2] Similarly, in the following year he praises another transatlantic novel for belonging to a school of American fiction 'characterised by a certain allusiveness of presentation which contrasts not unpleasantly with the directness of the ordinary English treatment, and enables us to apprehend a character by what may be called its aroma rather than its outline'.[3] However, Noble's reservation in 1881, that 'plot interest is not altogether contemptible', though mildly expressed, never disappears from his own critiques of the new school, and by 1885 he can show sympathy for those readers who are 'pining for nutriment a little more savoury than the long-drawn-out analyses of Messrs. Howells and James'.[4] Noble's conclusion, that the necessary 'sense of imaginative satisfaction' can only come from a boldly-defined plot 'with a fore-ordained and inevitable close',[5] indicates the rock upon which the English critics' faith was founded, and where Henry James's subtle vessel came to grief.

IV. UNITY OF STRUCTURE

Many of the contributors to this long dispute over plot and character seem at times to have assumed that the novel consists of various independent parts. The theory that challenges this is best known today (inevitably, it seems) as Henry James's:

[1] lvi (1899), 532–3.
[2] *Academy*, xx (1881), 397–8.
[3] ibid. xxii (1882), 394.
[4] ibid. xxvii (1885), 147.
[5] ibid. xxx (1886), 24. See also Noble's *Spectator* reviews above, pp. 50, 110–11.

> . . . this odd, literal opposition of description and dialogue, incident and description, has little meaning and light. People often talk of these things as if they had a kind of internecine distinctness, instead of melting into each other at every breath and being intimately associated parts of one general effort of expression. . . . A novel is a living thing, all one and continuous, like every other organism, and in proportion as it lives will it be found, I think, that in each of the parts there is something of each of the other parts.[1]

But the Master was not really alone in the wilderness. Important as his statement was, it would have been familiar to many readers and critics before 1884. In fact, the deliberate application of the principle of organic unity is one of the most remarkable and unexpected features in the whole age's criticism of fiction.[2] The assumptions about the detachability of plot and character, incident and description, are quite desultory beside it, and are less a theory in opposition to it than a simple failure of some critics to apply it fully or consistently.

The cry for 'relevance', 'design', and 'interdependence' is a loud one from the very first. Even when the phrases are brief and the metaphors simple, the cumulative effect is irresistible. 'Subordination or Proportion' is the quality essential to any novel, according to the *Westminster* in 1868; and it castigates the introduction of an irrelevant character.[3] In the same year the *North British* criticizes Hawthorne for a deficiency in 'architectural structure', and for treating each of the elements of his story in detail instead of all together: 'There is a want of the converging unity which is the condition of every perfect work of art.'[4] James Payn's *Walter's Word* is held up in 1875 as an example of proper construction: '. . . each separate portion of the plot fits into the rest, each successive situation arises naturally

[1] 'The Art of Fiction', *Longman's Mag.* iv (1884), 511.

[2] cf. Ford Madox Ford's typical dismissal of all that had gone before Conrad: '. . . what the Typical English Novelist had always aimed at—if he had aimed at any form at all—and what the Typical English Critic looked for —if ever he condescended to look at a novel—was a series of short stories with linked characters and possibly a culmination.' (*Return to Yesterday*, 1931, p. 208.)

[3] xxxiv, n.s. (1868), 576.

[4] 'Nathaniel Hawthorne', x, n.s. (1868), 191–2 (by 'Bell').

out of the others, and the further we read the more we are satisfied that the author has kept his work in hand and never lost sight of his original design.'[1] And one test for unity that critics frequently suggest is the effect of removing any one part of the work. The *Saturday* gives a good example of this in 1871 which also illustrates the concern felt for constructive standards in general:

No scene should be given in a novel which has not a direct relation to the conduct of the story, or the development of the characters. A novel should be like a puzzle, in so far that each smallest portion should have both its relative and absolute value; and it should be so closely welded that it would lose meaning, completeness, and consecutive interest, if only one of the smallest portions was taken away. But the great mass of novels are knocked up anyhow, obeying no rules of art worth speaking of, and certainly in complete disregard of this rule of interdependence. One might prune them of whole chapters and leave no gap; on the contrary, the story would be made more compact by the excision and brought into closer line.[2]

Other terms used to describe this 'consecutive interest' include 'dramatic *ensemble*' (in which, for example, Shorthouse's novels are lacking[3]); 'architectonics' (which Meredith, according to Macneile Dixon, only partly observes[4]); and a neologism of Saintsbury's, 'clip', describing the peculiar unity which 'keeps the characters of a novel together, and makes them fit into their places. . . . Without it, everything becomes episodic and vague, and one is constantly wondering why A appears, why B speaks, and why the book itself begins or ends as it does.'[5] But the most common images are those of a chain, and of weaving. In 1867 the *Westminster* insists that 'Each chapter in a novel should be a link in the chain'[6]; and in 1868 the *Spectator* laments: 'Incidents, indeed, there are plenty, but they are loosely strung together, not woven into any sort of a plot.'[7] Two later examples

[1] *Saturday Rev.* xl (1875), 438–9.
[2] xxxi (1871), 346–7.
[3] *Saturday Rev.* lxii (1886), 725–6.
[4] 'The Novels of *George Meredith*', *Quarterly Rev.* clxxxvi (1897), 160–1.
[5] *Academy*, xi (1877), 113.
[6] xxxii, n.s. (1867), 597.
[7] xli (1868), 76–77.

are enough to show how the same analogies appear ceaselessly throughout the period: R. D. Blackmore's *Springhaven* in 1887 'has many threads which are not properly interwoven, but dangle loosely about'[1]; and in all the novels of F. W. Robinson in 1890, 'the story unfolds itself coil after coil with a logical steadiness that nothing disturbs.'[2]

In the middle and later years, specific references to the novel as an organism, with the traditional Romantic metaphors drawn from botany and biology, become more and more common.[3] In 1873 the *Westminster*, for example, praises Miss Thackeray for her grasp of 'that which is the art of all arts, an organic fusion of the incidents into one living whole'[4]; and three years later the *Saturday* compares the novel 'to a growth where each preceding part is of vital importance to that which follows'.[5] In 1893 and 1894, in the *Spectator*, J. A. Noble's insistence on unity is satisfied by the way Conan Doyle makes each situation 'a nidus containing the germ of the situation that is to follow',[6] but is disappointed by Meredith's lack of 'organic integrity' ('The one thing needful in a novel is that it should be a whole.').[7] And Hardy's own principle—'Briefly, a story should be an organism'[8]—is confirmed by Lionel Johnson in his eulogy of the Wessex novels in 1894: '. . . phrase and scene and dialogue, incident and narrative and meditation, like the members of a body, do their part in their several places, for the general and common good.'[9]

Some critics, anxious to scotch any Romantic ideas of unconscious spontaneity in the artist that might lurk behind the

[1] *Spectator*, lx (1887), 391–2 (by George Hooper).

[2] *Athenaeum*, 1890 (ii), 93.

[3] The organic conception of the work of art is characteristic of Romantic aesthetics, but Victorian ideas of unity in the novel—for example, in the continual insistence that it should have a clear beginning, middle, and end—also owe something to the classical Aristotelian unity first claimed by Fielding and his contemporaries.

[4] xliv, n.s. (1873), 258. [5] xli (1876), 564–5. [6] lxx (1893), 811.

[7] 'Mr. George Meredith and Others', lxxiii (1894), 146–7.

[8] 'The Profitable Reading of Fiction', *Forum*, New York, v (1888), 66.

[9] *The Art of Thomas Hardy*, 1923 edn., p. 66.

organic theory, added a corrective analogy from painting, considered to be one of the more 'conscious' of the arts. In 1882 Mrs. Craik, for example, recommends that in novel-writing a central but unobtrusive 'idea' should give unity to the whole, like the spine of the body, or the trunk of a tree, holding together plot, characters, incidents, and conversation: 'All are sequences, following one another in natural order; even as from the seed-germ results successively the trunk, limbs, branches, twigs, and leafage of a tree.' But this simile from the natural world, she adds, should not conceal that the novel is a deliberate work of art, in which each effect, like the painter's, must be consciously achieved:

Every part should be made subservient to the whole. You must have a foreground and background, and a middle distance. If you persist in working-up one character, or finishing up minutely one incident, your perspective will be destroyed, and your book become a mere collection of fragments, not a work of art at all. The true artist will always be ready to sacrifice any pet detail to the perfection of the whole.[1]

More specifically, the doctrine of structural unity resulted in criticism of two familiar features in the Victorian novel, natural description and multiple plot. The excess of the former was an obvious object for attack. Enthusiastic reviewers of a different opinion quote 'gems' of description by such favourites as William Black and R. D. Blackmore till their page resembles a combination of holiday brochure and gardeners' catalogue; but there are many others, just as persistent, who declare that such passages must be made closely relevant to the whole book, and that sunsets over the Hebrides, in the Black style, are of no artistic merit in themselves. The *Westminster*, taking 'scenery' as one of the accepted components of the novel (even superior to plot) believes in 1876 that it must be used in sympathy or in contrast with the characters and actions: as an instance, the traditional sort of love-scene is more effective in an autumn landscape than in the midst of a storm.[2] And George Eliot is

[1] *Plain Speaking*, pp. 166–9.

[2] 'Ouida's Novels', xlix, n.s. (1876), 362–3.

praised five years later for observing 'the laws of poetic biology' in her descriptions of place: '. . . the correspondence between the material scenery, and the mental configuration, is a witness to the unity and genuineness of the creative impulse.'[1]

George Eliot fares less well in the critics' insistence that sub-plots, if allowable at all, should be very closely linked to the main action—*Middlemarch*, foreseeably, often being singled out for criticism. Earlier, George Venables finds fault with *Felix Holt* for a similar reason, and complains that Esther Lyon is the only liaison between the affairs of the hero and those of the Transomes: 'The story has the defect of running in two parallel lines with only an occasional and arbitrary connexion.' And the author has failed to realize that 'art compensates for its inability to copy the multiplicity of Nature by deliberate attention to unity'.[2]

Trollope is another offender who is frequently tasked with endangering the wholeness of his novels by spreading the interest over several plots. The *Saturday* condemns *The Vicar of Bullhampton* for 'showing no connexion whatever between the two trains of events and two groups of characters which occupy its pages'[3]; and the *Dublin Review* expresses disapproval for his manner of tearing the reader away from the main thread of the story to other figures only slightly connected with it.[4] Whether or not he always observed his theory, Trollope's own words on this matter are, as always, fair and reasonable, and indicate how the Victorian novel's comprehensiveness was to be made compatible with the laws of unity:

There should be no episodes in a novel. Every sentence, every word, through all those pages, should tend to the telling of the story . . . yet it may have many parts. . . . There may be subsidiary plots, which shall all tend to the elucidation of the main story, and which will take their places as part of one and the same work,—as there may be

[1] 'George Eliot: Her Life and Writings', *Westminster Rev.* lx, n.s. (1881), 175 (by W. M. W. Call).

[2] 'Felix Holt, the Radical', *Edinburgh Rev.* cxxiv (1866), 442–4.

[3] xxix (1870), 646–7.

[4] 'The Novels of Anthony Trollope', ix (1883), 327.

many figures on a canvas which shall not to the spectator seem to form themselves into separate pictures.[1]

One of the most interesting writers on the question of structure in the novel is George Moore, despite his eccentricities in other respects. His pronouncements on the technique of fiction are centred on the notion of organic unity, and sum up much of the fragmentary theorizing of others. Most often, his ideal is expressed in terms of music—the perfect image for formal proportion. He marvels at the complex interweaving of *L'Éducation Sentimentale*, at the continual subordination of the casual and particular phenomenon to the general conception, the avoidance of any disruptive sense of finality at the end of each episode or chapter: 'The texture is woven as closely as the music of "Tristan"—echoes, transformations, modulations, never a full close, always a suspended cadence.'[2] Again, in criticizing the disjointed structure of Olive Schreiner's *Story of an African Farm*, he defines the art of a novel as 'rhythmical sequence of events described with rhythmical sequence of phrase', and cites the tragic sense of inevitability that unifies *The Mill on the Floss*: '. . . that rhythmical progression of events, rhythm and inevitableness (two words for one and the same thing).' By emphasizing the need for synthesis, Moore succeeds in reconciling the various elements of fiction. Plot and character, for example, are inseparable: '. . . the sublimation of the *dramatis personae* and the deeds in which they are involved must correspond, and their relationship should remain unimpaired. . . . In the novel the characters are the voice, the deeds are the orchestra.' In the romances of Scott and Lytton, this is maintained—the chords are simple but perfect—but the modern romancers, the Haggards, Besants, and Christie Murrays, mix the modes of

[1] *An Autobiography*, 1883, ii, 56–58 (Chapter 12).

[2] 'A Tragic Novel', *Cosmopolis*, vii (1897), 49–50. He also uses 'instrumentation' to describe the novelist's device of blending physical phenomena from the outer world with the inner feelings of characters at some moment, as in Flaubert and Turgenev—'*des questions de métier*, but very interesting to those who would look behind the scenes and understand a little of the art of fiction' ('Turgueneff', *Fortnightly Rev.* xliii, n.s., 1888, 244).

realism and romance in such a way that the balance breaks down, and Trollopean characters are placed in Hugoesque situations: '. . . the result is inchoate and rhythmless folly, I mean the regular and inevitable alternation and combination of pa and ma, and dear Annie who lives at Clapham, with the Mountains of the Moon, and the secret of eternal life.'[1]

The false ending—a speciality of the English novelist—is another result of a breach in unity, a flaw in the sequence of events. The end of *Far From the Madding Crowd*, for example, is beneath contempt, according to Moore, and Hardy is never able to weld all the disparate lumps of his material into such a unity as *Silas Marner*; while the happy conclusion to Miss Thackeray's *Story of Elizabeth* is a 'dissonance', because the book has not succeeded in passing by any ingenious 'chords' out of its dominant 'key' of tragedy.[2] An example of the perfect ending is in Dostoevsky's *Poor Folk*, where a skilfully controlled anti-climax, like the use of the minor key, prolongs the melancholic effect of the whole book.[3]

Apart from this, Dostoevsky's novel provides an example of another kind of unity which Moore cannot find in English or French fiction. Its various threads of plot-contrivance are completely hidden, and exist only within the unified *impression* given by the whole work: 'The vulgar mechanism of preparatory scenes is withdrawn, is concealed in the things themselves, and so inherent and so complete is the logical sequence, that we are unconsciously prepared for each event; vulgar foreshadowing is unnecessary, and we watch the unfolding of the story as we watch the unfolding of rose leaves.'[4]

The last phrase gives a clue to Moore's strength and to his weakness as a critic of the novel. His perceptions are at times acute and original, but they are never followed up with much rigour. He is a novelist, responding with sensitivity to the practice of other novelists, and his comments are often better suited

[1] *Confessions of a Young Man*, 1888, pp. 278, 280, 271–4.
[2] ibid. pp. 266–70, 280–1.
[3] Preface to *Poor Folk*, 1894, pp. xv–xvi.
[4] ibid. pp. xii–xiii.

to stimulate a fellow-writer than to form part of a full theory of fiction. The imagery of rhythm and harmony certainly hints at an important idea in aesthetics, but the idea is evoked rather than defined. Nevertheless, Moore's analysis of Zola's *L'Assommoir* in his favourite musical terms illustrates finally not only the indirectness of his method, but the richness it can achieve by implication:

I had read the 'Assommoir', and had been much impressed by its pyramid size, strength, height, and decorative grandeur, and also by the immense harmonic development of the idea; and the fugal treatment of the different scenes had seemed to me astonishingly new—the washhouse, for example: the fight motive is indicated, then follows the development of side issues, then comes the fight motive explained; it is broken off short, it flutters through a web of progressive detail, the fight motive is again taken up, and now it is worked out in all its fulness; it is worked up to *crescendo*, another side issue is introduced, and again the theme is given forth. And I marvelled greatly at the lordly, river-like roll of the narrative, sometimes widening out into lakes and shallowing meres, but never stagnating in fen or marshlands.[1]

The doctrine that all poetry aspires towards the condition of music was hardly unfamiliar in late-Victorian England, but Moore was alone in elaborating it quite so fully in the realm of prose fiction. In his celebration of the quality represented by melody and harmony, he gave the organic concept of the novel one of its most eloquent, if tantalizing, expressions.

Before 1900, opposition to views like Moore's generally takes the form of simple indifference or conservatism—two influences on criticism which cannot be underestimated even in the nineties.[2] A possibly more significant reaction against the idea of formal strictness in fiction remains merely latent—for example, in 1899 Arthur Symons, who was neither conservative nor indifferent, defended Balzac's lack of unity on the grounds

[1] *Confessions of a Young Man*, pp. 119–20.

[2] Cf. Desmond Pacey, who sees the decade as one of enlightened technical debate to which the advent of Conrad and Ford came as a fitting climax ('Flaubert and his Victorian Critics', *Univ. of Toronto Quar.* xvi, 1946–7, 83).

that the novel is a form which must reflect the disorder of human life.[1] The conflict between these two views comes to a head only in the new century, most notably in the skirmishing of Henry James and H. G. Wells.[2] As yet, the idea of fiction as an organic structure which James expressed and so many others shared is not seriously challenged, and remains in its essentials the characteristic theory of the time.

V. NARRATIVE METHOD: THE OMNISCIENT AUTHOR

For the most part, Victorian critics visualize only three categories of narrative-method: that of the omniscient author, who writes predominantly in the third person, perhaps with some first-person commentary of his own; the directly autobiographical method; and the epistolary method. This triad is traditional—it is outlined by Mrs. Barbauld as early as 1804[3]—but it is rare to find a full and explicit description of it. One of the few appears in Walter Raleigh's *The English Novel* in 1894. The first device, according to Raleigh, is that of the narrating author, as in Fielding, Scott, Dickens, and Thackeray: 'He is invisible and omniscient, a sort of *diable boiteux*, who is able to unroof all houses and unlock all hearts. . . . At a slight sacrifice of dramatic force the events of the story are supplied with a chorus, and at any time that suits him the author can cast off his invisible cloak and show himself fingering the "helpless pieces of the game he plays".' The second is to place the story in the mouth of one important character, which gives to the book a dramatic centre and unity, but brings obvious hazards and problems. Among these are the unnatural omniscience that must be given

[1] 'Balzac', *Fortnightly Rev.* lxv, n.s. (1899), 753.

[2] See *Henry James and H. G. Wells*, ed. L. Edel and G. N. Ray, 1958. Arnold Bennett also joined the fray, rallying to Wells's journalistic banner after an early flirtation with formalism—see *Arnold Bennett and H. G. Wells*, ed. H. Wilson, 1960.

[3] *Correspondence of Samuel Richardson*, ed. A. L. Barbauld, 1804, i, pp. xxiii–xxviii.

to the narrator; the necessity of his dwelling on past events and thereby losing his own present reality; and also, 'although the single point of view is valuable to evoke sympathy, it takes from the novelist the privilege of killing his hero'. Third is the device of letters, amply justified by Richardson's use of it as a vehicle for detailed analysis: 'This constant repercussion of a theme or event between one or more pairs of correspondents produces a structure of story very like *The House that Jack Built*. Each writer is narrating not events alone, but his or her reflections on previous narrations of the same events.'[1]

In general, Raleigh's first category, the omniscient author, is given much more attention by critics than the various problems of internal narrative. Authorial intrusion, a Victorian convention scorned as primitive by later theorists, was surprisingly controversial in its own time.

In its defence, first of all, there are a number of critics who accept the 'dear reader' technique as one of the legitimate devices and attractions of the novel-form. For example, the *North British Review* in 1866 lists George Eliot's habit of commentating like a Greek chorus as one of her great strengths, which, as in the case of Thackeray, gives her work its breadth and power[2]; and George Barnett Smith in 1873 mentions Thackeray's continual presence at our elbow as one of the main reasons for the success of *Vanity Fair*.[3] Leslie Stephen, after taking a similar pleasure in Fielding's interpolations,[4] later gives one of the most enthusiastic of all defences of the method —a naturally corollary to his beliefs that the quest for illusion is a fallacy and that the nature of the author is a central concern. He dissociates himself from the common attitude to George Eliot's intrusions:

[1] pp. 147–52. In 1913 Saintsbury repeats the same threefold division, and claims that 'a hundred critics' have attested to its comprehensiveness (*The English Novel*, 1913, pp. 89–90).

[2] 'George Eliot's Novels', vi, n.s. (1866), 214 (by H. H. Lancaster).

[3] 'The Works of Thackeray', *Edinburgh Rev.* cxxxvii (1873), 102.

[4] 'Hours in a Library. XIV.—Fielding's Novels', *Cornhill Mag.* xxxv (1877), 157.

We are indeed told dogmatically that a novelist should never indulge in little asides to the reader. Why not? One main advantage of a novel, as it seems to me, is precisely that it leaves room for a freedom in such matters which is incompatible with the requirements, for example, of dramatic writing. I can enjoy Scott's downright story-telling, which never reminds you obtrusively of the presence of the author; but with all respect for Scott, I do not see why his manner should be the sole type and model for all his successors. I like to read about Tom Jones or Colonel Newcome; but I am also very glad when Fielding or Thackeray puts his puppets aside for the moment and talks to me in his own person.[1]

Before this time, in 1857, Trollope had justified his own intrusiveness by outlining in Chapter 15 of *Barchester Towers* an interesting doctrine of the confidence that must exist between author and reader. According to this, it is more important that the reader should share in the creator's sense of superiority over his personages, and avoid the indignity of being duped, than that illusion or artificial suspense should be maintained.[2] But most later defences, like Stephen's, simply stress the pleasures of being in direct contact with a pleasant or intelligent personality. In 1889 William Watson, for example, also opposes the current reaction against George Eliot's choric habit by praising the quality of the comments she makes[3]; and H. G. Wells, in an anonymous review of Gissing in 1896, criticizes the new dramatic theory of fiction which forbids commentary and by which 'we are robbed of the personality of the author'.[4]

However, there is not a great deal of weight behind this favourable attitude, and most critics from the earliest years are firm in their opposition. Very often, intrusion is merely called 'disagreeable' or 'a defect in a work of fiction'; but there is also a more specific insistence that the novelist should stand to his characters in the same relation as the dramatist, allowing them

[1] 'George Eliot', ibid. xliii (1881), 154–5.

[2] The Oxford Trollope, 1953, i, 143–4.

[3] 'Fiction—Plethoric and Anaemic', *National Rev.* xiv (1889–90), 168.

[4] *Saturday Rev.* lxxxi (1896), 405-6 (identified in *Edwardians and Late Victorians*, ed. R. Ellmann, New York, 1960, p. 116).

to reveal their own natures independently, by action and dialogue. Typical of this are, in 1865, the *Dublin University Magazine*'s praise of a writer for investigating character and motive by 'the presentation of both in the attitude and through the colloquies of the *dramatis personae*',[1] and the *Westminster*'s point, in 1877, that 'We do not require to be told that so-and-so is a good man or a witty man; we want to feel his goodness and to hear his wit.'[2] This emphasis on 'presentment'—similar to James's on 'rendering'—often combines with the other objections to 'analysis' we have already seen. For instance, in 1871 the *Saturday* takes strong exception to psychological analysis not only on the familiar grounds of it being painful and inhuman but also because it involves the author stepping forward and adopting 'the showman method of treatment', like a phrenologist pointing out the bumps on a stucco head, instead of letting the characters declare themselves.[3] And the same magazine sees another advantage in the disappearance of the showman, in that it is the best way of preserving consistency of characterization:

> One of the chief difficulties in writing a novel is to make the sayings and doings of the characters in it consistent with what is set forth about them at starting. They are apt to be one thing when the author speaks of them in the third person, and quite another when they speak for themselves in the first. . . . For this reason we have always thought Miss Austen's method of simply announcing a character and leaving him to describe himself, not only the most artistic way of proceeding, but the safest rule for an inexperienced writer to adopt.[4]

Jane Austen, together with Charles Reade, are two authors continually singled out for their self-denial and their dramatic method of characterization.[5] Reade himself, as a dramatist *manqué*, always emphasizes the virtues of scene and dialogue, and in various places in his novels he appears, a little contradic-

[1] 'Another Cluster of Novels', lxv (1865), 573.

[2] lii, n.s. (1877), 274.

[3] xxxii (1871), 216–17.

[4] xxiv (1867), 24–25.

[5] e.g. 'Jane Austen', *Saint Paul's*, v (1870), 632; H. D. Traill, 'The Novel of Manners', *Nineteenth Century*, xviii (1885), 572; 'Mr. Charles Reade's Novels', *Saturday Rev.* liv (1882), 180–1; and Walter Besant, 'Charles Reade's Novels', *Gentleman's Mag.* ccliii (1882), 202.

torily, to warn the reader against expecting any analysis from the author.[1] Reade also warns against a slightly different infringement on the characters' dramatic integrity: the direct intrusion of the author not even to analyse them but to philosophize irrelevantly over their heads. He describes the faults of a manuscript novel submitted to him by a friend of the authoress: 'Since preaching and moralising and discussing in their own persons is the foible of bad novelists, let her pass all such passages through a sieve, excise what is not new and good, and if she has uttered a gem or two, let her look and see whether she can't make this or that character say it.'[2]

Understandably, this kind of criticism is often levelled at George Eliot, despite her own insistence on 'the power of dramatic representation'.[3] Monckton Milnes, for example, writes of *Middlemarch* in 1873: 'Strictly speaking, the writer should be as little seen in person in a novel as he would be in a modern drama, where he only gives the stage directions; but here the Chorus is too continually present, calling us away from the excitement and anxiety of the piece to the consideration of the eternal moralities and humorous contrasts of life.'[4] And similarly, George Meredith is aware in theory of the importance of the dramatic scene—as witness his criticisms while reader for Chapman and Hall[5]—but is pilloried on all sides for the interjections that abound in his novels. In *Sandra Belloni* (1864), he shows his unease at the method by addressing 'this garrulous, super-subtle, so-called Philosopher' who has become his master:

[1] e.g. *Griffith Gaunt*, Library Edn., 1896, p. 164 (Chapter 23); and *A Perilous Secret*, ed. cit. p. 42 (Chapter 5). The *Athenaeum* sees the contradiction in 1885, pointing out that despite his many hints on the novelist's art, 'It was not in Reade's nature to remember at his desk that the story-teller should never obtrude himself' (1885 (i), 438).

[2] Quoted in Léone Rives, *Charles Reade, sa vie, ses romans*, Toulouse, 1940, p. 223.

[3] e.g. her reviews in the *Westminster Rev.* x, n.s. (1856), 259, 574.

[4] 'Middlemarch', *Edinburgh Rev.* cxxxvii (1873), 262–3.

[5] See R. A. Gettmann, 'Meredith as Publisher's Reader', *Journal of Eng. and Germ. Philol.* xlviii (1949), 54–56.

He maintains that a story should not always flow, or, at least, not to a given measure. When we are knapsack on back, he says, we come to eminences where a survey of our journey past and in advance is desireable, as is a distinct pause in any business, here and there. . . . In vain I tell him that he is meantime making tatters of the puppets' golden robe—illusion: that he is sucking the blood of their warm humanity out of them.[1]

It is surprising how few make Meredith's simple point that illusion is often shattered by the convention of omniscience. Of course, it underlies many of the other criticisms, but rarely becomes explicit. One of the first occasions is in 1875, in a *Spectator* review of a novel by Mrs. Oliphant, and there is a significant lack of urgency in the criticism : 'Too fond also is she of writing of her characters as if she stood apart from them and was criticising their motives, a defect which is also conspicuous in Mr. Trollope. When the reader is absorbed in a story, the obtrusion of the author's comments destroys something of the illusion. But these are trivial faults.'[2] James Payn in 1880 gives a stronger warning against the loss of naturalness that occurs when the showman reveals himself[3]; but it is the *Westminster*, eight years later, which makes the elementary but vital point most clearly, in its praise of Maupassant's technique in *Pierre et Jean*. Using 'subjective' in the same sense as Maupassant, to describe the psychological analysis of characters by the author, the writer argues for the superiority of the 'objective' method:

In our opinion, the subjective is less telling and less artistic, not only because it makes the fictive scene less like real life, as M. de Maupassant justly observes, but because it seems as if the artist were displaying the machinery of construction, which it is the instinct of true art to conceal. It is as though an architect left up the scaffolding by means of which he had reared his building. The novelist should, no doubt, as it were, enter into his puppets, and work them from the inside, but it should seem to the spectators as if they worked

[1] Memorial Edn., 1909, ii, 483–4 (Chapter 44).

[2] xlviii (1875), 407–9 (by John Dennis).

[3] 'Story-Telling', *Nineteenth Century*, viii (1880), 94.

themselves. In fact, *illusion*, not reality, is, as M. de Maupassant has perceived, the true aim and end of the novelist.[1]

The importance attached by critics to the dramatization of character is confirmed by another complaint which is perhaps less concerned with narrative position than with the whole basis of character-creation: that is, when an author fails to dissociate his own nature from that of his personages, an intrusion as fundamental, if not as direct, as that of personal commentary. The *London Quarterly Review* faults Dickens in this respect in 1871, complaining that *David Copperfield* 'reiterates too constantly the personality of the author', and making the point that an author must feel himself into the independent life of his characters so closely that his own private personality becomes excluded from them.[2] R. H. Hutton, reviewing *Far From the Madding Crowd* in the *Spectator*, makes a common criticism of Hardy, that the rustic characters speak and think too obviously with the author's own subtlety: 'Mr. Hardy seems . . . constantly to be shuffling his own words or tone of thought with those of the people he is describing.' Not only does he comment in his own person, like George Eliot, but, as she never did, blends 'a good deal of this same style of thought with the substance of his drawings'.[3] And Henry James, finally, is several times criticized because his characters 'know all the time that Mr. Henry James is looking; they are not sufficiently disengaged and projected'.[4]

On these various grounds, then, the convention of the self-revealing author was no favourite of Victorian critics, who show far more awareness of its dangers than its advantages. By the end of the century, its outmodedness was taken as self-evident in many quarters, and it received little fresh discussion. The *avant-garde* minority regarded it openly as a relic of barbarism, and the young Arnold Bennett, finally, gives a representative expression of their contempt. In 1896 he tells how in conversation E. M. Symonds ('George Paston') has lamented the decline of the novel since Thackeray and George Eliot: 'She regretted the

[1] cxxix (1888), 538.
[2] 'Dickens', xxxv (1871), 283–4.
[3] xlvii (1874), 1597–9.
[4] *Academy*, li (1897), 256.

lapse of that custom which made it lawful for authors to intersperse their narratives by personal reflections, opinions, moralizings. In the case of a great author, she said, these constituted for her frequently the chief charm of a novel. Which shows that sensible people are capable of holding the most bizarre views.'[1]

VI. THE FIRST PERSON

The only types of 'dramatized', as opposed to authorial, narration which critics could generally recognize were the autobiographical and the epistolary: both of them, that is, narratives in the first person given by one of the characters in the novel. Among the many criticisms, this method also won its share of appreciation. The *British Quarterly*, for example, sees its advantages in Mrs. Craik's choice of a character like Phineas Fletcher, the invalid Quaker, to tell the story of *John Halifax, Gentleman*. His feminine characteristics and deficiencies of insight suit perfectly the nature of the authoress, who herself lacks close knowledge of such a masculine figure as Halifax, the hero. She not only conceals her deficiency but actually makes the reader remedy it: '. . . the reader knows that he sees the life of John Halifax through the mind of Phineas Fletcher, and therefore pictures it as fuller and stronger and more manly than it is.' Such a success is contrasted with Mrs. Craik's later *Lord Erlistoun*, where a sentimental story comes to us quite incongruously through a rough and commonplace narrator.[2] This

[1] *Journals*, ed. N. Flower, 1932–3, i, 11. For criticism in the same key, rejecting the method as outdated, without any new reasons why, see the praises of Flaubert in 'The Art of Fiction', *Saturday Rev.* lxxviii (1894), 530–1; in D. F. Hannigan, 'Gustave Flaubert', *Westminster Rev.* cxliv (1895), 383–92; and, with reservations, in Ernest Newman, 'Gustave Flaubert', *Fortnightly Rev.* lviii, n.s. (1895), 823.

[2] 'The Author of John Halifax', xliv (1866), 43–44, 49. Richard Stang takes this same article's remark that *John Halifax, Gentleman* could not have been told 'from another point of view' as a very early use of 'point of view' in the specialized modern sense established by Percy Lubbock and others (op. cit. p. 107). But this, perhaps, is to force a very ordinary phrase into a fashionably modern straightjacket.

advantage for a woman novelist of choosing a *persona* with her own social and psychological limitations is also recognized by Frederic Harrison, *à propos* of *Jane Eyre*:

The plain little governess dominates the whole book and fills every page. Everything and every one appear, not as we see them and know them in the world, but as they look to a keen-eyed girl who had hardly ever left her native village. Had the whole book been cast into the form of impersonal narration, this limitation, this huge ignorance of life, this amateur's attempt to construct a romance by the light of nature instead of observation and study of persons, would have been a failure. As the autobiography of Jane Eyre—let us say at once of Charlotte Brontë—it is consummate art.[1]

However, the critics are even more aware of the difficulties of placing such a burden on one character: for example, the need to make him attractive in himself, and to prevent him from completely dominating the other characters and events. The *Spectator* in 1870 criticizes the hero-narrator of William Black's *Kilmeny* because he becomes a free outlet for the author's subjectivity and sentimentality, and thereby is himself mawkish, unattractive, and too obtrusive:

The hero, we are told by Mr. Black, is a mere 'lens', though which the scenes of the story are surveyed; and let us add that he is very far indeed from an achromatic lens, and that the phenomena known as those of diffraction are exceedingly well marked in his case . . . but that he is made the 'lens' for some passages of beautiful and thoroughly poetical description, we cannot say we like the object-glass through which the image of the story is focussed for us at all.[2]

The self-exposition and continual presence forced on a character-narrator results in such books being called 'egotistic'. In 1877 the *Spectator* sees the avoidance of this impression as 'the chief test of the skill with which an autobiographical novel is written'[3]; and Trollope, in a letter of 1868, elaborates on 'egotism' and its no less irritating obverse:

[1] 'Charlotte Brontë', *Studies in Early Victorian Literature*, 1895, pp. 162–3.
[2] xliii (1870), 469–70. [3] l (1877), 762–3 (by Mrs. Cashel Hoey).

. . . it is always dangerous to write from the point of 'I'. The reader is unconsciously taught to feel that the writer is glorifying himself, and rebels against the self-praise. Or otherwise the 'I' is pretentiously humble, and offends from exactly the other point of view. In telling a tale it is, I think, always well to sink the personal pronoun. The old way, 'Once upon a time', with slight modifications, is the best way of telling a story.[1]

A more particular point made is that the autobiographical technique must be consistent with the general tone of the whole book, as in the *Spectator*'s objection to W. E. Norris's use of the first person in 1886:

Mr. Norris cannot identify himself sufficiently with any of his characters to act simply as his or her mouth-piece. He looks upon humanity from a standpoint that is not quite Goethe's, that is nearer Thackeray's than Goethe's; but, in any case, he sits up aloft somewhere, seeing his world go. It is a dangerous experiment for the master of a show of marionettes to identify himself with any one of them in particular.[2]

Saintsbury, admonitory as always, is particularly alert to the dangers of autobiography, especially loss of *vraisemblance* when the narrator has to acquire and convey information. Cherbuliez, for example, though usually successful in 'the indirect forms of narration'—such as the device of having one character write or confess to a friend—can slip up at times, as when he is forced to make the narrating hero or heroine eavesdrop, thereby forfeiting our sympathy and credence.[3] The problem is illustrated even

[1] *Letters*, ed. B. A. Booth, London, 1951, pp. 216–17. What Trollope and others meant by these two offences is illustrated in Esther Summerson's clumsy establishment of her own virtues in Chapter 3 of *Bleak House*: 'I have mentioned that, unless my vanity should deceive me (as I know it may, for I may be very vain, without suspecting it—though indeed I don't), my comprehension is quickened when my affection is. My disposition is very affectionate. . . .' And in her simpering modesty: 'It seems so curious to me to be obliged to write all this about myself! As if this narrative were the narrative of *my* life! But my little body will soon fall into the background now.' (New Oxford Illustr. Dickens, 1948, pp. 16, 26.)

[2] lix (1886), 1309–10 (by William Wallace).

[3] 'Victor Cherbuliez', *Fortnightly Rev.* xxiii, n.s. (1878), 257.

more clearly for Saintsbury by the familiar convention of the governess-narrator, as in a novel he reviews in 1874:

Only by a never-failing employment of the most ingenious artifices, is it possible to make personal narrative at once probable and interesting. . . . The spokesman in a novel should either be the central figure, or else should be supposed to know everything. Miss Rudd neither is the one, nor does the other. Consequently we are deprived of the necessary details and circumstances without which a story, unless it be in very exceptional hands, is sure to languish.[1]

Finally, R. L. Stevenson's reliance on the autobiographic method brings several interesting reactions. A review in the *Athenaeum* for 1893 contains one of the few wholly laudatory accounts of first-person narration, in which the writer points out that the device often gives a greater 'organic vitality' to a story than would be achieved by the usual kind of plot. In the case of *Kidnapped* and *Catriona*, varied and even discordant matter has been given a perfect 'unity of impression' simply by the unity of the teller's own life and character: 'By the historic method material so disparate as that contained in the story and its sequel could hardly have been held together, howsoever skilfully the working characters might be kept revolving round the hero as centre; but by the use of the autobiographic method the hero's own personality prevents that solution of continuity which is so fatal to a work of art.'[2] This kind of advantage is ignored by Saintsbury, who can see in *The Master of Ballantrae* only the difficulties (acknowledged by the author in the Dedication) of using such a stolid, unimaginative narrator as the steward, Mackellar. Saintsbury—in polar contrast to James, who saw difficulty of method as artistic salvation—cannot understand an author's burdening himself in this way: 'Scott knew that constant attention to a "problem" of this kind is apt to impede the march of the story.'[3]

[1] *Academy*, vi (1874), 479.

[2] 1893 (ii), 375–7. *Kidnapped* was one of the few specimens of the autobiographic novel to overcome Henry James's distaste—and then only by virtue of its belonging to 'the fantastic and the romantic' (*Letters*, ed. P. Lubbock, 1920, ii, 188–9).

[3] *Academy*, xxxvi (1889), 284.

BIRKBECK LIBRARY COLLEGE

Stevenson, of course, is perfectly aware of what he gains by the method. He tells Gosse in 1893: '. . . the difficulty of according the narrative and the dialogue (in a work in the third person) is extreme. That is one reason out of half a dozen why I so often prefer the first.' And he describes how such a third-person narrative in *The Ebb-Tide* has resulted in 'strain between a vilely realistic dialogue and a narrative style pitched about (in phrase) "four notes higher" than it should have been'.[1] The use of Mackellar as narrator in *The Master of Ballantrae* has other merits, particularly that of providing a tactical distance: '. . . the device enabled me to view my heroine from the outside, which was doubly desirable. First, and generally, because I am always afraid of my women, which are not admired in my home circle; second, and particularly, because I should be thus enabled to pass over without realisation an ugly and delicate business—the master's courtship of his brother's wife.' The demerits, Stevenson admits, are that the melodrama of the conclusion comes awkwardly through such a medium as Mackellar, and that there is a loss of 'large dramatic rhythm'. But the verisimilitude that the point of view brings is its greatest virtue: 'The realism I love is that of method; not only that all in a story may possibly have come to pass, but that all might naturally be recorded—a realism that justifies the book itself as well as the fable it commemorates.'[2]

The epistolary form, not surprisingly, receives little attention from later Victorian critics, except as a narrative-method of historical interest. Most attempts to revive it are treated as anachronistic: 'With all reverence to the memory of Richardson, and not forgetting George Sand's incomparable *Marquis de Villemer*, and other five or six of her best works, we cannot help thinking that the epistolary form of romance has had its day.'[3] The memory of Richardson, in fact, sparks off most references

[1] *Letters*, ed. S. Colvin, 1911, iv, 179.

[2] 'Note to "The Master of Ballantrae" ', *Works*, Vailima Edn., 1922–3, xxvi, 480–1.

[3] Linda Villari, 'Novelists and Novel Writing in Italy', *Macmillan's Mag.* xxxviii (1878), 23.

to the method—especially at the time of Eneas Sweetland Dallas's abridged edition of *Clarissa* in 1868. They can be divided into those which disapprove on the expected grounds of the convention's 'unreality', and those which find, like the *St. James's Magazine*, that 'this epistolary style constitutes one of the chief charms of the book'.[1] Harry Buxton Forman and Leslie Stephen, as we have seen before, are both unconcerned about the improbability of the method. Forman points out that it allows greater psychological analysis, and that it purifies the more disgusting aspects of the story by bringing them to us 'polarised through the medium of Clarissa's noble and lucid mind'.[2] And Stephen praises the effect of persons revealing themselves without external analysis or description, and being seen from more than one angle: the reader thereby arrives at an intimate knowledge of both characters and events, built up with the minute accuracy of a Dutch painting. On the debit side, however, is the spectacle of characters trumpeting their own virtues, a difficulty which can be only partly overcome by the expedient of admiring confidants, as witness *Sir Charles Grandison*.[3] The same mixed view, finally, is taken in 1869 by the *Westminster*, which detects the improbabilities and incongruities, but goes on to praise Richardson's method as 'precisely the proper vehicle for his minute Prae-Raphaelitism in descriptive narration. To show the same characters and the same events in several lights, according to the personal quality of the narrator, was one of the leading principles of his method.'[4]

VII. 'INDIRECT AND OBLIQUE'

For Henry James, the perfect angle of narration lay somewhere between the two we have seen, the dramatized view-point of the autobiographer or letter-writer on the one hand, and, on the other, the undramatized 'mere muffled majesty of irresponsible

[1] 'Richardson's "Clarissa" ', ii (1868-9), 252.

[2] 'Samuel Richardson, as Artist and Moralist', *Fortnightly Rev.* vi, n.s. (1869), 433–4. See above, pp. 44, 46.

[3] 'Richardson's Novels', *Cornhill Mag.* xvii (1868), 55–57.

[4] 'Richardson's Clarissa', xxxv, n.s. (1869), 55–57.

"authorship" '. James came to aim at an account in the third person in which an impersonal author is rigidly subjected to 'the register, ever so closely kept, of the consciousness' of a limited number of the characters, thereby producing 'a certain indirect and oblique view'.[1] The major difference in the conception of 'point of view' is that for James it is determined mainly by the centre of awareness, and, for most other critics, simply by the centre of articulation: that is, whether the words of the narrative are 'spoken' by a character or by the author.

There are only two accounts which hint at an idea similar to James's. One of these, an interesting article by Paul Bourget in the *New Review* for 1891, suffers from some confusion. Bourget dislikes the objective method of Flaubert and Turgenev, which, he says, consists of the author mistakenly 'effacing himself behind his hero, so that his own impression does not influence the reader's . . . he is like a watchmaker who has made a watch'. Yet his description of the so-called subjective method which he prefers shows that it can include not only the familiar first-person commentator like Stendhal and Balzac, but also what he apparently dismissed before, a completely dramatized vantage-point restricted to one character and told in the third person. In his first phrase, 'effacing himself behind his hero', Bourget probably means not the dramatized point of view but, more simply and more generally, an author's lack of imaginative involvement with his characters. However, his disapproval of Tolstoi's avoidance of a central figure leads to a less ambiguous description of the point at issue:

He does not reflect that those events would not be the subject of a narrative if they were not known, and that they can only be known by the intellect which classifies them in becoming acquainted with them. Hence is derived that great principle which the classical masters have never disregarded, the subordination of the characters, and the central position given to one of them, from whose point of view all the others are seen.[2]

[1] Preface to *The Golden Bowl*, in *The Art of the Novel*, London, 1935, pp. 327–9.

[2] 'The Science of Fiction', iv (1891), 306–7.

The second article is one which contains not only a full exposition of point of view in its modern sense, but is in many other respects one of the most remarkable of all late-Victorian pronouncements on the craft of fiction—and one that appears to have gone largely unremarked. The frequent appearance of the name of Vernon Lee (Violet Paget) has already testified to her interest in the novel, and her 'On Literary Construction', in the *Contemporary* for 1895, is the work of one who has thought deeply about the specifically technical problems of the novelist's art.[1] Many partial anticipations of Henry James's later criticism are obvious—and, as regards her occasional obscurities and contradictions, it should be remembered that James's own treatment of point of view is far from clear, and needed the later exegeses of Lubbock and other disciples.[2]

Starting with the simple but vital proposition that the art of fiction consists in manipulating the reader's mind by the arrangement of words, Vernon Lee proceeds by stages which deserve to be looked at in detail. Her original conception of the novel as a structure of devices is illustrated at once by an analysis of how Stevenson uses a small and gruesome episode near the beginning of *Catriona* as a qualifying adjective on a large scale, in order to establish a certain state of mind in the reader rather than to advance the 'events'. A novel, she suggests, is written like a series of interacting themes in a symphony or opera, each description, or line of argument, or character, producing a planned and related effect in the reader. A diagram drawn to illustrate the progress of any novel's complex of thoughts, moods, groups of facts, etc., should be a perfect circle or ellipse: only this way,

[1] lxviii (1895), 404–19. The essay, along with several others already referred to, was republished in *The Handling of Words* in 1923, a book which has received some notice in general terms; but the significance of her early articles on the novel has never been recognized, even in Peter Gunn's recent *Vernon Lee* (1964).

[2] She and James enjoyed a fairly close acquaintance from the seventies or eighties until a breach in 1892. See C. J. Weber, 'Henry James and his Tiger-Cat', *P.M.L.A.* lxviii (1953), 672–87; and B. Gardner, 'An Apology for Henry James's "Tiger-Cat"', ibid. pp. 688–95.

by the organic inevitability of form, will the reader's mind be mastered and led along the intended path.[1]

Having established organic unity and the reader's responses as her basic principles, Vernon Lee then examines the question of narration. She criticizes the confusion that results from the fragmented method, as in the opening of *Wuthering Heights*, and also the mechanical ease of the old autobiographical method, which imposes unity in a crude fashion. Much more mature is to arrange the characters and events as in real life and change the point of view from one figure to the other. One method of third-person narrative is also strongly criticized, one which she holds to be typical of the English three-volume novel: '. . . the dodge of arranging the matter as much as possible as in a play, with narrative or analytic connecting links.' This scenic method fails because the play, unlike the novel, is essentially non-naturalistic, and also because the introspective or self-assertive temperament implied in characters who are frequently presented *en scène* is often contrary to the impression of them conveyed by the narrative portions. 'Scenes', as in the case of Tolstoi, should be ancillary and infrequent, always dependent on the primary motive power of 'the force of accumulated action'.[2] Other draw-backs of the dramatic method are the need to insert background description by narrative; the invention of minor characters in order to elicit the main characters' qualities; and the proliferation of episodes simply for this purpose: '. . . meanwhile the real action stops; or, what is much worse, the real action is most un-naturally complicated by such side business, which is merely

[1] See also her analysis of 'style' in terms of psychological manipulation in 'The Craft of Words', *New Rev.* xi (1894), 571–80: '. . . the construction of a whole book stands to the construction of a single sentence as the greatest complexities of counterpoint and orchestration stand to the relations of the vibrations constituting a single just note.'

[2] She shows some confusion here over the definition of the 'scene'. In her praise of Tolstoi's avoidance of it, it clearly means the big *scène à faire* of passionate dialogue and critical action—'dramatic' in the idiomatic sense. Yet the 'scenic method' she disparages also seems by her description of it to include any dramatized presentation of characters thinking or acting—which is plainly Tolstoi's method in *Anna Karenina*.

intended to give the reader information that he either need not have at all, or ought to get in some more direct way.'

After further criticism of the devices of 'retrospects' and 'foreshortening' made necessary by the scenic method, and both destructive of unity, Vernon Lee comes to the kernel of the matter: the angle of narration. The passage must be quoted at length to illustrate how fully the idea was developed by this critic twelve years before James's famous Prefaces to the New York Edition, and twenty-six before Lubbock's *The Craft of Fiction*:

There is yet another constructive question about the novel—the most important question of all—whose existence the lay mind probably does not even suspect, but which, I am sure, exercises more than any other the mind of any one who has attempted to write a novel; even as the layman, contemplating a picture, is apt never to guess how much thought has been given to determining the place where the spectator is supposed to see from, whether from above, below, from the right or the left, and in what perspective, consequently, the various painted figures are to appear. This supreme constructive question in the novel is exactly analogous to that question in painting; and in describing the choice by the painter of the point of view, I have described also that most subtle choice of the literary craftsman: choice of the point of view whence the personages and action of a novel are to be seen. For you can see a person, or an act, in one of several ways, and connected with several other persons or acts. You can see the person from nobody's point of view, or from the point of view of one of the other persons, or from the point of view of the analytical, judicious author. Thus, Casaubon may be seen from Dorothea's point of view, from his own point of view, from Ladislaw's point of view, or from the point of view of George Eliot; or he may be merely made to talk and act without any explanation of why he is so talking and acting, and that is what I call nobody's point of view.

The latter is usually the case in adventure stories, where the chief interest is in incident rather than psychology; but beyond that level, the question of Whose point of view? becomes unavoidable.

Although like any good theoretician Vernon Lee allows each method its merits, she more than hints at a preference when she goes on, characteristically, to relate the choice of point of view to the psychology of character-creation. She divides novelists into the synthetic, who feel their characters intuitively, and mysteriously give 'birth' to them; and the analytic, whose characters are more consciously evolved, and become 'illustrations of theories of life in general' or of the life of certain classes and temperaments'. The latter will prefer the external point of view of the 'judicious author'; but the former (*pace* Paul Bourget in his *New Review* article) will prefer the alternating point of view of 'straightforward narrative', which is really the temporary but total identification of the author with each personage through a sense of love, or sometimes (as in James's Olive Chancellor) an equally creative sense of hate. The supreme example is once again her beloved Tolstoi, 'who in his two great novels really *is* each of the principal persons turn about; so much so, that at first one might almost think there was no point of view at all'. When for the reader the point of view seems to disappear, then for the writer it is supremely at work, and his Protean triumph is complete.

In some ways, Vernon Lee's theory is more comprehensive and more sympathetic than James's, which makes such a high virtue out of economy, and in its application tends to follow Narcissus rather than Proteus. But a more incontestable and more relevant point is that her article deserves to rank beside any single similar piece of writing by James for its qualities of originality, reasonableness, and devotion to the craft of novel-writing. Although in detail it is hardly typical of its era, its general concern for artistic unity and for the novelist's best use of the means peculiarly at his disposal—for construction as a discovery of what precisely he 'can afford and cannot afford to do'—connects it with all that was most scrupulous and most alert in Victorian criticism of fiction. The plea with which it closes might be taken as the simplest justification and creed of all the host of critics whose ideas we have been examining—all the critics, famous or forgotten, who grappled with the youngest, most perturbing, most dominating art-form of their century:

> . . . the small fragments of literary or artistic faculty which we all are born with . . . can be increased and made more efficient only to a limited degree. What we really have in our power is either to waste them in cumbering the world with work which will give no one any pleasure, or to put them to the utmost profit in giving us the highest degree of delight from the work of those who are specially endowed. Let us learn what good writing is in order to become the best possible readers.

LIST OF PERIODICALS

It would be impracticable to give here a list of all the Victorian periodical articles, reviews, and books, and of all the modern works relevant to the history of novel-theory, which have been consulted for this study. It is hoped that the index, the details in the footnotes, and this list of periodicals actually mentioned in the text, will serve to indicate major sources of information.

The Academy
The Argosy
The Athenaeum
Belgravia
Blackwood's Edinburgh Magazine
The Bookman
The British Quarterly Review
The Contemporary Review
The Cornhill Magazine
Cosmopolis
The Dublin Review
The Dublin University Magazine
The Eclectic Review
The Edinburgh Review
The Fortnightly Review
Fraser's Magazine
The Gentleman's Magazine
The Leader
Literature
The London Quarterly Review
London Society
Longman's Magazine
Macmillan's Magazine
The Magazine of Art
The National Review
The New Monthly Magazine
The New Review
The Nineteenth Century
The North British Review
Once a Week
The Pall Mall Gazette
The Quarterly Review
The St. James's Magazine
Saint Paul's
The Saturday Review of Politics, Literature, Science, and Art
The Savoy
The Scots (then *National*) *Observer*
The Spectator
Temple Bar
Time
The Times
Tinsley's Magazine
The Westminster Review
The Yellow Book

INDEX